THINE IS THE
KINGDOM

Also by Bishop Emmanuel Mc. Lorren,
Then Comes Revival,
Sound of an Abundance of Rain,
Living the Abundant Life through Divine Deliverance

THINE IS THE KINGDOM

Walking in Kingdom Mentality

Bishop Emmanuel Mc Lorren

Foreword by Rev. C. Natasha Sifflet

iUniverse, Inc.
Bloomington

Thine is the Kingdom
Walking in Kingdom Mentality

iUniverse books may be ordered through booksellers or by contacting:

iUniverse
1663 Liberty Drive
Bloomington, IN 47403
www.iuniverse.com
1-800-Authors (1-800-288-4677)

ISBN: 978-1-4620-3328-7 (pbk)
ISBN: 978-1-4620-3570-0 (ebk)

Printed in the United States of America

iUniverse rev. date: 06/24/2011

DEDICATION

To my wife Tara Mc Lorren, whose love and support for me is immeasurable; my daughter's able assistance in a nation transforming ministry and to all my spiritual children who have made me proud, as I see the image of Christ the King of glory, reflected in their character. It is also to the many students of Bethel Tabernacle's School of Ministry who have gotten hold of the revelatory truth of Kingdom Leadership.

CONTENTS

FOREWORD

Bishop Emmanuel Mc Lorren challenges individuals to seek first the Kingdom rule and authority of God, in their lives. He sets the atmosphere for the development of passion to be in the presence of the King of kings, who is Jehovah and helps to position believers, encouraging them to operate in Kingdom authority. Bishop Mc Lorren's unfolding of the King's favour and how to find it, places the ardent seeker right in the flavour of the favour of the Lord God Almighty. This revelation of sonship as stated in the book of Saint John, chapter one and verse twelve, "For as many as receive Him, to them He gave power to become the sons of God", brings every believer into a kingly inheritance. One who has gained the revelatory understanding of their kingly inheritance as stated in Romans chapter eight verse seventeen, will enjoy the bountiful blessings of the Kingdom of God. "And if children, then heirs; heirs of God, and joint-heirs with Christ; if so be that we suffer with Him, that we may be also glorified together".

In this literary piece, there is a clear ambassadorial vision which will develop, after understanding your royal position in Christ. The revelations of this book will undoubting, help you to live in the blessing and benefits of the kingly life, because in the presence of the Lord there is fullness of joy and at His right hand, there are pleasures forever more. Basking in the awesome revelation and truth that the King of kings watches over us with a jealousy eye, is amazing!

Thine is the Kingdom will cause you to be refreshed, re-focused and repositioned to operate in Kingdom authority!

Reverend C. Natasha Sifflet
Assistant Pastor Bethel Tabernacle, St. Lucia

PREFACE

Thine is the Kingdom was birthed from my Ministry's Vision (E & M Mc Lorren Networking Ministries International) "to reach generations with the life-changing power of the Gospel and to develop a holistic understanding of Kingdom living". Having served as pastor from 1979, I realize that many believers live below their God-given privileges as children and heirs to His Kingdom. Through the pages of *Thine Is the Kingdom*, the Body of Christ will be equipped to understand their role, and fulfill their purpose in God's Kingdom. My hope is that through this study, many will shift from the futuristic concept of the Kingdom, which has its place, to practical everyday Kingdom living.

The history of the Church and its forward progression of world events, is heading to a climatic end with eschatological phenomena and catastrophic disasters on earth, as God Almighty puts down rebellion, and establishes His eternal Kingdom. *Thine is the Kingdom* is not seeking to present a theological discourse on the Kingdom of God or the rule of God, but is seeking to bring proper spiritual perception concerning the rule of God on earth at this present time and season. It draws from the Biblical based teachings of the Apostles Paul and Peter, who in the Epistles, establish that, the children of God (those who have received Jesus Christ the Prince of glory) have passed from death unto life: Ephesians 2:18, "For through Him (Jesus Christ) we both have access by one Spirit unto the Father. Now therefore ye are no more strangers and foreigners, but fellow citizens with the saints, and of the household of God." The Apostle Paul boldly declares the believers' present position in Ephesians 1:3, as being blessed with all spiritual blessings in heavenly places in Christ.

The Apostle Peter in his clarion call to Kingdom realization and practical living said, "but ye are a chosen generation, a royal priest hood, an holy nation, a peculiar people; that ye should shew forth the praises of Him who hath called you out of darkness into His marvelous light" (1 Peter 2: 9-10). The Apostles and the other writers of the New Testament teach us that the new creatures in God have become Kingdom people. Jesus Christ himself said, "The Kingdom of God does not come with observation," because the religious people of His days were looking for some physical sign of God's Kingdom. He clearly states that the Kingdom of God is within us.

Jesus introduced the first phase of His mission on earth—to establish His Kingdom of God within the hearts of men. This concept was misunderstood by His followers. The leaders of Israel looked for a king who would ride on a horse, over-throw the Roman Empire and establish his throne in Israel. Many Bible commentators believe that one of the reasons why Judas chose to betray Jesus, was because he felt that if Jesus was placed in a precarious situation where He had to defend Himself against the Roman army, He would use the awesome power that He had manifest so many times, and lead an aggressive, forceful action against the Roman authority to establish His physical kingdom. But Jesus' teachings had a futuristic aspect of the Son of man coming back with an army of His saints to judge the wicked and rebellious kingdom, which is under Satan and his son of perdition the antichrist (the man of lawlessness).

Thine is the Kingdom will cause you to focus on the rule and dominion of God in the earth and in the hearts of men who have been regenerated by the power of the Blood of Jesus, making the believer the temple of the Living God. Every believer in this twenty-first century must enter into their Kingdom authority, living as a priest and king unto God until the King of kings physically returns to the earth. The King will first call unto Himself, His Kingly bride, and secondly establish His Kingdom on earth. Reading *Thine is the Kingdom* will cause you to be committed to God so that you will be among those that He calls unto Himself!

—Bishop Emmanuel Mc Lorren

INTRODUCTION

In the last half of the twentieth century, the Church of Jesus Christ experienced a structural change. The traditional Church began to experience a shift in ministry. Some ministry gifts which were considered to be irrelevant for the modern era were re-introduced to the Body of Christ. Some ministry gifts namely the Apostles and Prophets who were deemed not applicable to the Church were discarded. Strong theological positions which were carefully articulated by scholars who held dogmatic stances backed by volumes of carefully researched thesis, tried to stop the functions of these gifts but yet they emerged. The gifts that experienced a rebirth—so to speak—in the twentieth century were the ministry of the Apostles and Prophets.

Pioneers like Kenneth Higgins, Oral Roberts, and Bill Hamon, to name a few, went against the prevailing teaching of the day to bring the manifestation of these gifts to the pulpit of the Christian Church. This ministry restoration which began through the illumination of the Holy Spirit, which was preceded by ardent fervent prayer of prophetic and strategically placed intercessors in the Body of Christ, has come of age!

The Apostle Paul ceaselessly prayed for the Ephesians Christians, Ephesians 1:16-18;

> "Cease not to give thanks for you, making mention of you in my prayers, that the God of our Lord Jesus Christ, the father of glory may give unto you the spirit of wisdom and revelation in the knowledge of Him, the eyes of your understanding being enlightened, that ye may know what is the hope of His calling and what the riches of the glory of His inheritance in the saints and

what is the exceeding greatness of His power towards us who believe, according to the working of His mighty power."

This specific prayer pattern no doubt was circulated throughout many nations of the world. Through intense intercessory prayer for the restoration of the gifts which have come to be known as the five-fold ministry gifts, which the Apostle Paul addressed in Ephesians 4: 8-16, the Church is better positioned to reach maturity and do the work of ministry. The Living Bible states, "The Psalmist tells about this for he says that when Christ returned triumphantly to heaven after His resurrection and victory over Satan He gave generous gifts to men. Notice that it says He returned to heaven. This means that He had first come down from the height of heaven, far down to the lowest parts of the earth. The same one who came down is the one who went back up, that He might fill all things everywhere with Himself from the very lowest to the very highest." The King James Version of the Bible Ephesians 4:11; "and He gave some apostles and some prophets; and some evangelists; and some prophets and teachers." The gifts were given by Jesus Christ the head of the Church which is the Body of Christ, for the perfecting of the saints for the work of ministry, for the edifying of the Body of Christ.

This twentieth century surge, awakening and restoration of spiritual gifts is definitely necessary so that the Body of Christ could develop into its full potential. My prayer is that the ignorance that was taught in the church through the spirit of error is dissipating.

Thanks to God for the awareness that is now permeating the Body of Christ, there definitely is overwhelming evidence that the five-fold ministry gifts are now accomplishing its God-given purpose.

Peter Wagner calls the paradigm shift in the Body of Christ a 'church-quake'. He sighted that there has been a greater emphasis on the believer's position power of the Holy Spirit within the church, the principles of faith and teaching of healing, and many other truths that have been revealed. It seems that the focus on

Jesus' return to earth and the urgency of preparation for the return of King Jesus has shadowed the Church's need for occupying in Kingdom authority now on earth.

The Church must refocus on a concept and philosophy, that seeks to transform nations from the kingdom of darkness to God's Kingdom of Light, preparing the Body of Christ for the return of the King, bringing ordinary believers to Kingdom understanding, thinking, and mentality, which is necessary so that the gates of hell will not prevail.

Chapter 1

Why Kingdom Mentality?
Pursuit of purpose demands Kingdom mentality

Kingdom transformation and replacement seems to be the focus and the centre of Jesus' teaching. In the gospels, Jesus discussed the Kingdom of God dozens of times. God's original idea concerning rule on earth was kingdom rule. The Creator established earth as an extension of His universal Kingdom. God extended His Kingdom rule through man on earth. His original plan for man was, and still is kingdom life; God's original purpose for man is ruler-ship dominion.

Man's constitution reveals his kingly nature. It's not by mistake that Revelation 5:10 states, "You have made them to be a kingdom and priests to serve our God, and they will reign on earth" (New International Version). In Revelation 3:21 Jesus promised the over-comers of the Laodicea church to sit with Him on His throne. "To him who overcomes I will give the right to sit with Me on my throne, just as I overcame and sat down with My father on His throne."

In Revelation 20: 1-6 the great dragon, the ancient serpent the devil, Satan, is seized by an angel and is bound for a thousand years. Verse four of Chapter twenty in the book of Revelation, reveals thrones on which were seated those who had been given authority to judge. In the book of Revelation we see the original purpose of God realized and reestablished; redeemed man sitting on thrones, judging and finally becoming a kingdom of priests to serve our God—their reign is on earth!

The Apostle Peter receiving the revelation of man's kingly and priestly position wrote under divine unction, "But you are a chosen people a royal priest hood, a holy nation a people belonging to God, that you may declare the praises of Him who called you out of darkness unto His wonderful light" (1 Peter 2:9).

God's original intended purpose for man will be accomplished, fulfilled and realized, because man's full potential and fulfillment is wrapped up in his purpose and assigned destiny.

Man of purpose: The book of Genesis 1:26; "Then God said, let us make man in our image in our likeness, and let them rule, subdue, have dominion over fish of the sea, birds of the air, over live stock, over all the earth and all the creatures that move along the ground."

God created man to have dominion over the earth as the only legal authority. The word dominion speaks of having sovereignty—sovereign control of territory. Human beings are the legal authority on earth. The word human is a composition of the words humus, which means dirty and organic constituent of soil, and man, a spirit being. God said let there be light and there was, he said let us make man and let them have dominion over all the earth. Adam fell from dominion authority when he disobeyed God who had delegated earth's authority to him. Mankind lost their authority to rule and subdue, and subsequently Satan took control by default.

Man's failure to fulfill his obligation to rule, through his disobedience, fell from grace which is the unmerited favour of God, and came short of the glory of God. Man fell from royalty and divine presence and became slaves to Satan and the earth which he was created to subdue and rule.

Kingly restoration demands or necessitates the actions of kingly seed. Jesus' journey to earth was to reestablish kingly rule to man. Jesus' heavenly origin (Jehovah is savior) and His journey from the centre of the throne and the existence of God, the I am (the self existing One), the Most High God made Him the right person to restore man to kingly position. The book of St. John in the Bible, chapter one and verse one describes Jesus as the Living Word. "In

2

the beginning was the Word and the Word was with God and the Word was God."

The Apostle John expressed that Jesus is Creator, John 1:3 "Through Him all things were made, without Him nothing was made that has been made." The Apostle in the first Epistle of John 1:2 said, "For the life was manifested, and we have seen it, and bear witness, and show unto you that eternal life, which was with the Father, and was manifested unto us."

The Bible clearly showed Jesus' earthly kingly heritage. The scepter, a symbol of kingly rule came out of Judah. Moses the exodus leader of Israel said in Numbers 24:17. "A scepter shall rise out of Israel and shall smite the corners of Moab, and destroy all the children of Sheth." This scripture refers to the coming of Christ the Messiah. Psalm 45:6 declares the scepter of thy Kingdom is a righteous scepter. Hebrews 1:6 states, "And again, when God brings His first-born into the world, He says, Let all God's angels worship him."

In Psalm 45:7 the psalmist speaking of angels said, "He makes His angels winds (spirit) His servants flames of fire". In verse eight of this same Psalm, He states, "But about the Son He says, your throne O God will last forever and ever, and righteousness will be the scepter of Your Kingdom." King Adam lost his kingdom rule and dominion through pride and disobedience. King Jesus re-gained earthly rule for man through obedience and humility—Philippians chapter two verses five to ten.

First John Chapter three verse eight says, "He that commits sin is of the devil, for the devil sinned from the beginning. For this purpose was the Son of God, manifest (revealed, appear on earth), to destroy all the work of the devil". First Corinthians two and verse eight reminds us that none of the rulers of Jesus' age understood. For if they had known, they would not have crucified the Lord of Glory.

Jesus Christ through the process of the cross, reestablished kingly rule and dominion to man and made this declaration in Mathew 16:18; "And I say unto thee, That thou art Peter, and upon this rock I will build my church; and the gates of hell shall not prevail against it." Having accomplished the task according to the book of Colossians 2: 15 states ("And having disarmed the powers and authorities, He made a public spectacle of them, triumphing over them by the cross"), Jesus Christ in bold declaration of conquest, after His resurrection, stated in Mathew 28:18 ". . . All power is given unto Me in heaven and earth." In pursuit of purpose we must be transformed into kingdom mentality.

Chapter 2

Building in Kingdom Mentality
Kingdom mentality demands Kingdom thinking

"God's ultimate goal for your life on earth is not comfort, but character development", Rick Warren, Purpose Driven Life. You were created to become like Christ.

The Apostle Paul said that Jesus gave gifts to the Church. His intention was the perfecting and full equipping of the saints (God's consecrated people), that they should do the work of ministry towards building up Christ's body the Church, that it might develop until we all attained oneness in the faith, and in the comprehension of the full and accurate, knowledge of the Son of God, that (we might arrive) at mature manhood (The completeness of personality which is nothing less than the standard height of Christ our perfection), the measure of the stature of the fullness of Christ and the completeness found in Him.

Dear reader as Christians we are not members of a social club, we are not just denominational people; we are called to partake in the divine nature. We were created to be like Christ; from the very beginning, God's plan has been to make you like His Son Jesus. This is your destiny and the third purpose of your life—the first is worship that gives glory God, the second is to rule and have dominion on earth.

Becoming like Christ:

The Apostle Paul in Ephesians 4:22-24; points out our third purpose—becoming like Christ. For the believer to make the

5

transition from church member to kingdom movers and shakers, he or she must choose to let go of old ways of acting, and everything connected with that old way of life. It is necessary that there be a change in the way we think; it is written in the Holy Scriptures, "As a man thinketh in his heart so is he" (Proverbs 23:7 King James Version). We must allow the precious Holy Spirit to change the way we think. The Bible clearly states in the book of Romans 12:2, "and be not conformed to this world but be ye transformed by the renewing of your mind, that ye may prove what is that good, and acceptable, and perfect, will of God".

The Greek word for "Transformation", Metamorphosis, used in Romans 12:2, and 2 Corinthians 3:18; is used to describe the amazing change a caterpillar goes through in becoming a butterfly. It is a beautiful picture of what happens to us spiritually when we allow God to direct our thoughts; we are changed from inside out.

Spiritual growth and mind transformation is not automatic, it takes an intentional commitment. The individual must want to grow, decide to grow, make an effort to grow and persist in growing.

Change your life, by changing your auto pilot:

To change your life you must change the way you think. Most of us have our thought life on auto pilot, preprogrammed thoughts and fixed patterns which most time are misguided, ill-informed, worldly and sensual. We are told that behind everything we do there is a thought, as a man thinks in his heart so is he, and from the abundance of the heart the mouth speaks. Dr Myles Monroe says, "That there is nothing as powerful as an idea; it is the most powerful component on earth. An idea is a thought, a thought is a silent word, a word is an expressed thought; words are thoughts' containers, everything starts with a thought". Because of the nature of thoughts, the Holy Scripture warns about idle words. Jesus said that for, "Every idle word we speak we will have to give an account, but I tell you on the Day of Judgment men will have to give account for every idle (inoperative, non-working) word they speak" (Mathew12:36). This scripture tells us that words are important to

God, He takes words seriously. The power of words was clearly demonstrated in Jesus' earthly ministry; He cast out devils with words, He stilled the storms with words, the Jews said never had they heard a man speak like Him.

Through the prophet Isaiah, God clearly states to the children of Israel, "For my thoughts are not your thoughts neither are your ways my ways declares the Lord, for as the heavens are higher than the earth so are my ways higher than your ways and my thoughts than your thoughts. God's Word shall not return void but shall accomplish that which God speaks" (Isaiah 55:8-9 paraphrased). Man speaks useless, idle, vain babbling, old wives' fables and snare themselves, because the power of life and death is in the power of the tongue (Proverbs 18:21). God does not say anything He does not mean and He means what He says. God created everything by His word.

Hebrews 11:3 (Amplified version)

"By faith we understand that the worlds (during the successive age) were framed (fashioned put in order, and equip for their intended purpose) by the Word of God, so that what we see was not made out of things which are visible."

Behaviour is motivated by belief, and every action is promoted by an attitude. God revealed these truths thousands of years before psychologists understood these facts of the universe.

Be careful how you think, your life is shaped by your thoughts, be careful what you say, your words are expressions of your thoughts, and as a man thinks in his heart so is he. Let God transform you into a new person by changing the way you think. Your first step to spiritual growth is to change the way you think and change always starts in the mind. Therefore you should be careful about the way you think because it will determine the way you feel, and the way you feel influences the way you act.

The Apostle Paul advocates strongly that there must be a spiritual renewal of thoughts and attitude, to be like Christ the (anointed one), the King of kings. We must cultivate the mind of Christ, through a mental shift which is called repentance, which in the Greek literally means, "to change your mind". You know that you repent when you have changed the way you think by replacing your thoughts with God's thoughts concerning sin, God himself, other people, life, your future and everything else, taking on Christ's outlook and perspective.

Kingdom thinking is essential to spiritual growth:

We are commanded to think the same way that Christ Jesus thought. Philippians 2:5a "Let the same mind which was in Christ be in you". This mental shift demands a stop in thinking patterns of immaturity, which are self-centered and self-seeking. The Apostle Paul said to stop thinking like children, but with regards to evil be infants, but in righteousness be adults, because selfish thinking is the source of sinful behaviour. Maturity starts with thinking maturely which focuses on others, not you, thinking of others is the mark of maturity.

1 Corinthians 13:11

"When I was a child, I spake as a child, I understood as a child, I thought as a child: but when I became a man, I put away childish things."

Dear reader let God Almighty change you through His Word inwardly, by a complete change of your mind. Then you will be able to know the will of God, what is good and is pleasing to Him and is perfect. In Romans 2:2b the Apostle Paul encourages the Philippians' Christians to think on, "Whatsoever things that are true, whatsoever things are honest, whatsoever things are just whatsoever things that pure, whatsoever things are lovely, whatsoever things are of good report; if there be any virtue, and if there be any praise think on these things" (Philippians 4:8).

In 2 Peter 3:1 the Apostle Peter stimulates the believer to wholesome thinking, understanding that Kingdom mentality demands a removal of hindrances to Christ-like, kingdom thinking.

Chapter 3

Kingdom Discipline
Indiscipline in the Church is a hindrance to Kingdom life

The topic of church discipline is not a popular one, but it is very important for the church to consider. Sadly, many have shied away from this discussion however for the church to maximize its full potential and become what Christ Jesus intended for it, discipline is a must.

The Apostle Paul through divine revelation wrote to the Ephesians Christians about the hope of their calling in God, and their position in Christ. The Apostle previewed the Church as a finished product, which Christ Jesus bought with His own precious blood (sanctified by the washing of the water by His Word) to present it to Himself a church without spots, wrinkles or blemish.

In this paper we will define the Church, as God established it to be, making reference to the children of Israel in the Old Testament as God's called-out ones. The paper defines the term "the church" using the Hebrew word Rahall (or Kahal) coming from the root word meaning "to summon" as "assembly" or congregation, and the Greek equivalent, 'Ekklesia' coming from two Greek words: 'Ekk' meaning 'out of' and 'kaleo' meaning 'to call'.

The background of the usage of the word in a Greek culture is closely examined, which gives great insight and a clear understanding of the cultural understanding in Jesus' days on earth. The writers quoted in this paper have many years of experience in Church ministry and therefore help to put the question of Church discipline in the right context, dealing with the need for discipline in the Church. The discussion covers paid workers, volunteer workers and membership.

A clear definition of Church discipline is stated, highlighting that Church discipline, must be a system which disciples, trains and administers rules and punishment to deviant behaviour.

The Lord Jesus Christ's idea of the Church is much different from what we have today in many circles of Christianity. The Lord's understanding of Church, as expressed by the early Church community has been lost in today's modern society. There is a need for the Christian community to rediscover the true meaning of the word Church as the Lord Jesus Christ intended in Mathew chapter sixteen verses seventeen to nineteen.

Background:

As I further discuss the concept and meaning of the word "Church", I will, in this section, make reference to quotations and teachings from Kervin J. Conner.

Kervin, J. Conner, said, "The word Church is a word which has lost most of its meaning today in comparison to what it originally meant in the early Church times. It is a word that needs to be re-defined in our modern society. There are a number of organizations and groups in existence today called "the church", but they are certainly not that which the Lord Jesus Christ said that He would build."

As we seek to understanding and define the Church, it must not be mixed with the concept of material building of stone or wood. The Church is God's master piece of earth and part of the Kingdom of God.

Concerning the word "church", Conner also said "The word church is never used in scripture to refer to a material building. The word "church" is used about one hundred and forty times in the New Testament, but never once used of a material building of wood or stone."

To truly understand the purpose of a thing we must go to the beginning of the thing, consulting the maker or creator. The Church is no exception to that principle. There are words in the Greek language that gives to us the root meaning of the word Church. As we examine the term "The Church" we will find out that the concept was a prevailing concept in Jesus' days on earth, especially among the hierarchical system of Greek and Roman society.

Conner further said that the "Greek background of the word 'church' in the Apostle Paul's day is seen in the following: In the great classical days of Athens, the "Ecclesia" was the convened assembly of people. It consisted of the entire citizen who had not lost their civic rights. Apart from the fact that its citizen had to conform to the laws of the state, its powers were to all intents and purposes unlimited."

The "ecclesia" of the Greek/Roman world, enjoyed tremendous privilege, but seemed to have had immense responsibilities as citizen. Kervin, J. Conner listed some of those responsibilities:

(a) Their elected and dismissed magistrates
(b) Direct the policy of the city
(c) Declare war, made peace, contracted treaties and arranged alliances
(d) Elected generals and other military officers
(e) Assigned troops to different campaigns and dispatched them from the city
(f) Ultimately was responsible for the conduct of military operations
(g) Raised and allocated land

He concluded, "thus for the secular Greek society, the word "Ecclesia" came to mean assembly of free citizen who were called out of their homes and or places of business to assemble together and to give consideration to matters of public interest."

The understanding we get from the original, cultural meaning of the word "church" from the Greek secular society, shows vast differences in contrast to what we call "church" today in many places. The concept of a called-out group of people managing the affairs of a kingdom is clearly seen in the operation of the Church.

Definition:

To have a clear understanding of what the Church is to do and be, one must know what the Church is. Terry, L. Gyger says, "We must first understand what the church is before we can know what it is to do and how. In the Bible the indicative always precedes the imperative, what the church is, stands before and points to what the church is to do."

W. Barclay gives some excellent information concerning the true meaning of the word "church" he says, "The New Testament word for Church is a most important word in New Testament words. It has a double background and it comes from two Greek words: Ek meaning 'out of' and Kaleo meaning "to call"; the Hebrew word Qahal (or kahal), coming from the root word "to summon" as "assembly" or congregation." The author notes that "the Hebrew word for church occurs over seventy times in the Septuagint. In the Hebrew sense it means God's people called together in order to listen to or act for God." Surely this definition further clarifies the word Church and gives a picture of an authoritative disciplined community of life-changing, Kingdom people who truly reflect the Church that our Lord Jesus Christ said that He would build.

The Holy Scriptures teaches clearly that discipline in Church should not stop at preaching behind pulpits, but should be enforced within the community of believers. In many church communities that I am familiar with, discipline seems to be non-existent.

Discipline in some church groups is left to the local pastor of that community of believers. The Holy Scripture statement in the book of Mathew chapter eighteen verses fifteen to eighteen includes the entire Christian body in the task of maintaining discipline in the Church.

As a result of the low levels of discipline within the Church, the Church is weakened from within. The effectiveness of the Church is compromised on the altar of tolerance, which gives way to bad character, lack of integrity and morality which do not reflect the principles of the Kingdom of God, which is moral excellence, integrity of character.

Definition:

In defining Church discipline, it must be considered as a system which disciples, trains and administrates rules and punishment to deviant behaviour. Ray C. Campbell says, "The word discipline means:

(a) Teaching, learning, to disciple;
(b) Training that connects, molds or perfects the mental faculties or morals;
(c) Punishment to inflict pain or penalty
(d) A rule or system of rules which governs conduct or activity."

The Need for Discipline:

It is a fact that for any organization, firm, club, charitable organization and church group to grow and be effective, there must be systems of discipline. These systems of discipline should be stated clearly in the core values of that organization, spelt out in its operational and governing policy, so that the congregants and workers both paid and volunteer can be guided and reprimanded when necessary. Haddon W. Robinson, says, "Just as ancient athletes discarded everything and competed naked, so must the disciplined Christian divest himself of every association, habits and tendency which impedes godliness."

Hughes says that, "Discipline is essential to accomplish anything in life, but we must avoid legalism and judgmental behaviour. We will exercise discipline because we love God and want to please Him." Just as discipline is essential to achieve anything in life, so must it be operative in the life of the Church if it is going to be successful.

The question is asked by a leadership journal in an article on building Church leaders, "Can you discipline a volunteer"? What is the Biblical pattern for dealing with a destructive volunteer? How does Matthew chapter eighteen verse fifteen, work in the situation of disciplining volunteers? The dynamics of volunteer workers poses a serious challenge when it comes to disciplining major. Unless the volunteer sees his or her self as working for God, and is accountable in the final analysis to Him, but also is accountable to human leadership over them, the volunteer worker will find it difficult to receive discipline at the hand of leaders and fellow workers. Volunteerism comes with a demand for appreciation from leadership or fellow members. Volunteerism faces the constant threat of mediocrity and lack of professionalism. As a result of the absence of monetary compensation, due to the inability of the Church to pay wages, there is a high tolerance of deviant behaviour among volunteer workers. It must be understood that Matthew eighteen addresses every member of the Body of Christ.

Motive of Church discipline:

It must be stated clearly, that while Church discipline must not be compromised through fear and indifference, discipline must be administered with the right motive, not for personal vendettas, in love, and appear to be just.

Ray, C. Campbell says, "The motive of Church discipline is to maintain order. First Corinthians chapter fourteen verse forty says, "Everything must be done decently and in order." To improve performance (2 Corinthians 7:8-11), to prevent deterioration (1 Corinthians 4:6-8), to correct, undesirable behavior, and to restore (1 Corinthians 5: 1-13; 2 Corinthians 2: 6-11; Galatians 6:1)."

Mac. Arthur, F. John, Jr. outlines the elements of Church discipline to be:

1. The place of discipline in the church;
2. The purpose of discipline to restore;
3. The person of discipline, considering the object of discipline as a child of God, and a human being with feelings and needs;
4. Provocation of discipline through deviant behavior;

5. The process of discipline, clearly defined rules, and consequences; and

6. The power of discipline to maintain scriptural order, to elevate standards within the Church community and to serve as deterrent to deviant behaviour.

Motivation a deterrent to indiscipline:

In many disciplines of life, motivation is used as a means of keeping discipline in behaviour and production, through human resources department. The Church, though its work force is primarily volunteers, must employ motivational programs to serve as deterrents to indiscipline. There is a growing need for the Church to arise to fulfill its purpose, find its identity and heritage, and walk in its potential in God. The Church must see herself as Kingdom people with a divine destiny as their goal. Every member must realize that they belong to a Kingdom that is superior to all earthly kingdoms. Born again believers must know who God is: a God of design and objectivity Who does everything well. The child of God must strive for excellence and defy indiscipline and mediocrity.

Discussion:

In examination of the evidence before us, we must agree that the Lord Jesus Christ intended that His Church be a well disciplined, body of believers, with purpose, destiny and authority. The reality we face in our churches is defiant to what God's Word explains and declares in Matthew eighteen verses fifteen to nineteen, Mark sixteen verses fifteen to twenty and Acts two verses two to four.

The pragmatic philosophy and contemporary theological position that deviates from the scriptural absolute, for instance the issue of gay marriage among clergy, has made the Church vulnerable to indecent behaviours. The push to make the Church user friendly, by creating a 'non-offensive and loving environment', has opened it to high levels of indiscipline.

The fears of law suits, in the case of disgruntled members who are subject to disciplinary action, continue to hinder leaders from taking principled Biblical disciplinary action. The lack in disciplinary action by the Church has not helped to bring change and maturity in the way the Jesus Christ envisaged it to be. Instead we have developed a group of people who are not disciplined in their devotion to God, in marriage, speech, commitment to service, in dress code and behaviour. This situation of indiscipline needs to be addressed, though difficult because of the varied views which now prevail in Christendom, especially among the born-again group of believers.

The growing impact of globalization and culturalization on world thinking, which are not necessarily theologically sound, are pushed through the media, Hollywood and the music world, seem to set the trend which many Christians follow.

The time has come for the Church to come back to Bible basics, back to the principle of God's Kingdom, walking circumspectly not as fools but as wise. There is a call to redeem the time because the indiscipline in the Church seems to equal or surpass the conditions in the Corinthian Church, which the Apostle Paul called carnal and babes in the Christian walk, because of the indiscipline behaviour, and immorality that prevailed in that church.

A conscious decision of will must be made from top to bottom in restoring discipline in the Church. The Church must reflect the image of Christ and respond to the Word of the Lord to be holy as He is holy.

Chapter 4

The Mind of Christ and Kingdom Mentality
Ministering the Mind of Christ results in Kingdom Mentality

Dr. Bill Hamon outlines in his teaching on ministering the mind of Christ, what he calls five scriptural minds in the Holy Scriptures, namely:

1. The spiritual mind;
2. The soulish mind;
3. The natural mind;
4. The carnal mind; and
5. The mind like the soils of the earth.

To minister the mind of Christ which in fact is ministering in Kingdom mentality, warrants that we understand the Scriptural minds and their attributes which Dr. Bill Hamon elucidated in his book on spiritual gifts.

The Spiritual Mind:

The child of God is called to operate with a spiritual mind. The Apostle Paul exhorts the Corinthian Christians to walk in the spirit, shunning carnality and embracing maturity. For the Christian to walk in the path way to maturity, he or she must recognize and clearly understand that his or her thoughts must originate from the Anointed One, the risen Christ. To have the mind of Christ which results in Kingdom mentality, the child of God must submit him or herself to divinely inspired thoughts or impressions, which are definitely rooted in the Word of the Lord.

The born-again believer must avoid ministering at all times to please the flesh or to satisfy the man. He or she must realize that all the glory goes to the Lord of Hosts and minister from the depths of his redeemed spirit, allowing his spirit to become the candle of the Lord. The Christian walk is designed to be controlled by the Spirit of God. In the book of Romans 8:14, we are told, "As many as are lead by the Spirit of God are the Sons of God". The book of Galatians chapter five and verse twenty-four, writes that if you walk in the Spirit you shall not fulfill the lust of the flesh. One of the prevailing problems of the Church is immaturity which is the result of carnality, selfishness, divisiveness and personal-kingdom building.

A carnal life does not showcase the principles of the Kingdom of God. On the contrary, the spiritual mind highlights God's Kingdom principles. The Lord Jesus Christ in high priestly role, and apostolic mission on earth demonstrated the principles of His Father's Kingdom, clearly stating that in His Kingdom those who have reached the coveted position of leaders are the greater servants. This was a sharp deviation from the worldly view of his time, where the masters lord themselves over their subjects. Jesus also taught His disciples that they should beware of the leaven of the Pharisees, which meant do not pattern your life after the traditional living of hypocrisy, which is solely an outward show but inwardly they were filled with all sorts of carnality.

Jesus also taught that the confession of the mouth must correspond with relevant action, saying in Matthew chapter seven, "It is not those who say Lord, Lord that shall enter to the Kingdom of Heaven but those who do the will of My Father." Jesus boldly declared that His meat was to do His Father's will, stating that as He sees the Father work, so He works also. Jesus said that He must do the will of Him that sent him; at the garden of Gethsemane, in the deepest agonizing moment of His life on earth He said, "Father if it is possible let this cup pass from me, but not my will but thine be done." Jesus Christ personified the Kingdom of God's principles and lifestyle in His daily walk on earth, so must every Christian allow the Kingdom principles of God to prevail in his or her life on earth, as Christ's body, His Witnesses and His Ambassadors.

The Soulish Mind:

For spiritual growth and to develop a Kingdom mentality—the guides into Kingdom thinking which manifest Kingdom principles, we must clearly understand the soulish mind as stated in 2 Corinthians 10:5 "Though we walk in the flesh, we do not war after the flesh; for the weapons of our warfare are not carnal but mighty through God to the pulling down of strong holds." The soulish mind seeks to combine the natural and the spiritual, which is often the case in the Body; this in itself is old teachings of Gnosticism.

The Apostle Paul wrote to address that teaching in the Roman church, in his book to the Romans saying, "To be carnally minded is death but to be spiritual minded is life and peace through Jesus Christ our Lord", stating emphatically that he that is in the flesh cannot please God. The soulish mind has the ability to imagine and produce self-motivated ideas which does not bring glory to God. This soulish mind is sensitive, to one's own intuition, has a tendency to lean on gifts and above normal special abilities. There is a constant desire to control and direct the ministry of the Holy Spirit. It is also seen in cases where Bible knowledge is dispensed without the wisdom of God or the presence of a spiritual mind. This soulish mind is clearly seen when divine things are used for selfish purposes, or manipulating others by using spiritual abilities.

The Natural Mind:

The third mind that must be examined is the natural mind, which produces normal thoughts that are neither good nor bad. These thoughts are produced through secular education, formal or informal. The mind is trained and skilled to operate in a certain manner, hopefully to benefit the individual and for the good of mankind. The natural mind gives the ability to live and function. This natural mind controls the center of the human body.

The Carnal Mind:

The fourth mind to be considered is the Carnal mind. The Apostle Paul addressed the Corinthians, Romans and Galatians Christians on the issue of carnality in the Church, using scriptures like:

* Romans 8:6-7
* 1 Corinthians 3:1-4
* Galatians 5:19-21

He clearly stated that there is a battle raging on the inside of man between the spirit and the flesh. The Apostle encourages the believers to seek to walk in the spirit not after the flesh, or with a carnal mind which is enmity against God. As we carefully observe the attributes of the carnal mind, we realize that the thoughts of that person, originates from the lust of the flesh. The Apostle John wrote in his epistles to the Diaspora, "Love not the world neither the things that are in the world because all that is in the world is the lust of the flesh, lust of the eye and the pride of life". The beloved Apostle realized preoccupation with the worldly, carnal things identifies and activates the works of the flesh.

The born-again Christians fall prey to the works of the flesh through preoccupation with the world's system, which automatically influences their thinking and thus their actions are fleshly instead of spiritual. This concept is illustrated in the dress-code of Christians, which is heavily influenced by some designer in Holly Wood or some popular music superstar. It should be modest with the understanding of not being salacious, but bringing glory to God.

The carnal mind is consumed with sensual and evil thoughts that are sometimes demonically inspired. The Apostle Paul wrote to the believers in:

- Romans 1:28
- Titus 1:16
- 1 Timothy 3:8
- 1 Timothy 4:2
- 2 Corinthians 13:5-7

He wrote these letters concerning the dangers of walking in a carnal state of mind, which can lead to a reprobate mind. A reprobate mind has to do with a seared conscience, the inability to receive the Word of God because of the absence of Holy Spirit's convictions. Let us take this warning seriously and consciously choose to be lead by the Spirit of God Almighty. Do not be hardened but be pliable in the hands of God, presenting our bodies as living sacrifices, holy and acceptable unto God. Be not conformed to the world but be transformed by the renewing of our minds, so that we might know what is the good, pleasing, and acceptable will of God, that we can serve Him in humility, according to the major of faith and grace He has given us.

Chapter 5

Kingdom Principles verses Lawlessness

God set laws and order in the universe, and set boundaries of operation on earth. There are natural laws in the earth that, when human beings violate them, there are inevitable consequences. For instance the law of gravity-which is a force of nature, when violated has devastating consequences.

By now we should have an understanding of the phrase "Kingdom of God" but for a clearer understanding, let us define the phrase "Kingdom of God". The word "kingdom" is made up of two words: a king rules and reigns and the king's Domain. "King's Domain" = King-Dom. It is the territory or area over which a king rules and reigns—the king's domain. God's Kingdom is the reign or rule of God, whether in heaven or earth. It is the purpose of God—the extension of God's rule.

The Greek word for 'kingdom' is "Basileia". It speaks of the sway, rule, and administration of a king; the royal reign of the Kingdom of God. One cannot separate the King and the Kingdom as far as God is concerned. The Kingdom of God is an everlasting Kingdom (Psalms 145:10, 13; 103:19; Daniel 4:3). There has never been a time when the Kingdom of God has not been in existence. It has neither beginning nor end. The Kingdom of God is sovereign, ruling over kingdoms (Psalms 103:19; Revelation 11:15). The Kingdom of God is all-inclusive, including within itself, its domain, the total universe, the elect angels, heaven, the fallen angels and all creatures and mankind on this earth. All are under His control and dominion. None could exist or act without His sustaining power (Psalms 103:19; Exodus 15:18, Psalm 145:10-13). Definition by

This book is focusing on the aspect of the Kingdom of God in Christ in relation to the Church Christ's Body on earth. As we search the pages of scripture looking at the kingly line coming from the son of Jacob, we see God preserving the House of Judah in the land of Palestine until the advent of the King, Jesus Christ. The Gospel of Mathew is the gospel of the King and the Kingdom. Jesus preached, taught and demonstrated the Kingdom of God. Jesus clearly gave the laws of the Kingdom in Mathew chapters' five to seven. He presented the rule and reign of God to the house of Judah (Mathew 4:17, 23-25). The King was actually the personification of the Kingdom of God in the earth.

- Jesus preached the Gospel of the Kingdom:

  Matthew 4:23
  Mark 1:14
  Acts 1:3

- Jesus taught the Kingdom of God was at hand:

  Mathew 4:17
  Mark 1:15.

- Jesus showed that His ministry ushered in the next stage of the Kingdom:

  Matthew 12:24-28
  Luke11:20; 16:16

Kingdom of God Kingdom of Heaven:

The Life Application Bible lists 32 Scriptural references dealing with various aspects of the Kingdom of God and the Kingdom of heaven. It must be noted that the terms are used interchangeably.

The explanation of the Kingdom is stated in Matthew 3:2; 4:17; Mark 10:37: Luke 9:11 and 1 Peter 2:11.

- Qualification to enter the Kingdom   -Matthew 5:3-12
- Past present future aspect
  of the Kingdom   -Matthew 6:10;
    Luke 4:43
- Not all who talk about
  it belong there   -Matthew 7:21
- The Kingdom has already begun
  in the hearts of believers   -Matthew 10:7;
-      John 3:3; Acts 1:6
- The Kingdom is explained
  in parables by Jesus   -Matthew 13:24;
    Mark 4:26-29
- From small beginning
  to great results   -Matthew 13:31-32
- It's worldwide impact   -Matthew 13:33
- It's priceless value   -Matthew 13:44-46
- Humans cannot judge
  who will be in it   -Matthew 13:47-49
- Why the religious leaders
  missed it   -Matthew 13:52
- Keys to the Kingdom given
  to Jesus' disciples   -Matthew 16:19
- Misconception about
  the Kingdom   -Matthew 17:22-23
- Membership rule of the Kingdom   -Matthew 20:1
- Importance of bearing fruit
  in the Kingdom   -Matthew 25:29-30
- Disciples will see it arrive   -Mark 9:1
- Why it is difficult for the
  rich to enter   -Mark 10:23
- Developing proper perspective
  of the Kingdom   -Mark 12:24
- Relationships in the Kingdom   -Mark 12:25-27
- Why it is good news   -Luke 4:43
- The Kingdom is both
  spiritual and physical   -Luke 9:2

- The Kingdom is equally
  available to all   -Luke 10:21
- How to make it your top priority   -Luke 12:31
- Jesus is preparing a place in the
  Kingdom for his own   -Luke 12:35
- Those in it may surprise us   -Luke 13:30
- Not fully realized until
  Jesus comes again   -Acts 1:3
- Do you really want it to grow   -Luke 19:20-27
- The Establishment of the
  Kingdom is a cause for joy   -Luke 19:39
- Do not let personal concerns
  blind you to its coming   -Luke 22:24
- Many thought that Jesus' death
  had finished it   -Luke 23:42-43
- Reversal of Kingdom values   -Luke 24:25
- God personally invites us
  into the Kingdom   -1 Corinthians 1:2

One may ask the question, how long has the Kingdom of God been in existence? The Kingdom of God is an everlasting Kingdom (Psalms 145:10, 13; 103:19; Daniel 4:3). There has never been a time when the Kingdom of God has not been in existence. It has never begun nor will it end. The Kingdom of God is all-inclusive, including within itself—its domain, the total universe, the elect angels, heaven, the fallen angels, all creatures and mankind on this earth. All are under His control and dominion. None could exist or act without His sustaining power (Psalm 103:19; Exodus 15:18, Psalms 145:10-13).

These scriptural positions and many others indicate imperatively that the Kingdom of God is properly organized, and operates on divine laws which are higher and above human relativity, tradition and pragmatic laws.

There are civil laws set by governments and kingdoms to preempt and deter lawless activities which are harmful to human beings. If these laws are ignored the penalties are handed down by the court system of a kingdom, a country or state. God the Sovereign Ruler of the universe has set laws in the earth realm. For instance, there are laws of increase set in the earth:

- Sowing and reaping;
- Seed time and harvest.

Genesis 8:22, "As long as the earth remains, seed time and harvest will be". When there is violation of the laws of seed time and harvest, sowing and reaping, poverty emerges or criminal activities become prevalent.

The principle of success, increase and prosperity once followed brings desirable results, while the sowing of bad seed result inevitably in destruction. The writer of the Psalms states in chapter one verses one to four:

> "Blessed is the man that walketh not in the counsel of the ungodly, nor standeth in the way of sinners, nor sitteth in the seat of the scornful. But his delight is in the law of the LORD; and in His law doth he meditate day and night. And he shall be like a tree planted by the rivers of water, that bringeth forth his fruit in his season; his leaf also shall not wither; and whatsoever he doeth shall prosper. The ungodly *are* not so: but *are* like the chaff which the wind driveth away". King James Version

God has set Spiritual laws which must be followed for success in life. These principle laws are summarized in the Proverbs, Song of Solomon and Ecclesiastes. Ecclesiastes 12:13-14

> "Let us all hear together the conclusion of the discourse. Fear God, and keep His commandments: for this is all man: And all things that are done, God will bring into judgment for every error, whether it be good or evil".

27

In the book of Proverbs we are told that the fear of the Lord is the beginning of wisdom, the person who fears God will be consciously aware of any violation of God's laws. In the book Exodus 20:1-17 the laws and commandment of God is introduced to Israel and by extension the human race. Jesus states clearly that it is not the professor of Christianity who says Lord, Lord that shall enter the Kingdom but those who do the will of the Father.

We are reminded that God will bring every work into judgment, including every secret thing (revealed of darkness and wickedness, secret sins, silent rebellion, hidden conditions in man's heart) because the heart of man, the Scripture declares, is desperately wicked—but God will judge.

The Apostle John tells us in John 5:24 that life and judgment are through the Son of God, Jesus Christ:

> "And all things that are done, God will bring into judgment for every error, whether it be good or evil. Verily, verily, I say unto you, He that heareth my word, and believeth on him that sent me, hath everlasting life, and shall not come into condemnation; but is passed from death unto life"

Modern civil society has found itself in a crossroad with four philosophical viewpoints pulling in different directions.

1. **Humanism:** With its pragmatic philosophical ideology, which projects the law of relativism and dismisses the very thought of absolutes, predicated on the principle if it feels good do it.
2. **Religious Idiosyncrasy:** Is the error of man's own making. This concept is driven by materialism.
3. **Satanism and Occultism:** Feeds on the quest and greed of the human as they seek to pursue power and wealth.
4. **Divine Law:** Almighty God's laws are imbedded in His Word, which is the answer to all mans problems, "But be seeking first the kingdom of God and His righteousness,

and all these *[things]* will be added to you." The kingdom of the earth is presently under the guidance and watchful eyes of the Creator of heaven and earth. We His created beings will do well to place ourselves under the guidance and tutorship of the Master and King of the universe.

Chapter 6

Thine is the Kingdom
The kingdoms of the earth have become the Kingdom
of our God and his Christ.

The battle for world domination by individuals, sects, countries, religious ideologies, human philosophy like Marxism, imperialism, capitalism, socialism etc. have seen many of the leaders and promoters of these concepts of government come and go from the world's scene.

The earth realms have been graced and disgraced by leaders like Alexander the Great—the Grecian conqueror, Napoleon Bonaparte—the French military general, Adolph Hitler—the German War chancellor, Starling—the Russian strong man and many more did reign over earth's affairs, as world changers, influencers, and conquerors of mighty armies, nation states and kingdoms, which were in many cases under servitude to these world rulers.

It must be noted that the mental accruement, military genius, and the persuasive eloquence of man does not preserve longevity, which helps us to understand that it does not matter how mighty, powerful and influential a man becomes, his reign on earth will come to an inevitable end. But the cycle of life continues. It is evident through historical records, artifacts and archaeological findings, that man's kingdom reigns continue to fail and cease to exist, because it is time bound.

The tower of Babel reminds us that man's best efforts will eventually fail in the face of divine purpose. Whenever man seeks to rule outside of God's ordained structure his establishment will eventually come crushing down. The magnificence and power of the Roman Empire, was brought to its knees as men refuse to acknowledge Jehovah. King Herod the Great was eating by worms when he delivered an oratory to move the multitudes to worship him as god. King Nebuchadnezzar of Babylon ate grass for seven years when he failed to acknowledge the hand of God in the building of the city of Babylon. Boastfully ignoring the warning of God in a dream,

"At the end of twelve months the king walked in the palace of the kingdom looking at the hanging gardens of Babylon and said, 'Is not this great Babylon that I have build for the house of the kingdom by the might of my power and for the honour of my majesty?', while the word was still in the king's mouth there fell a voice from heaven saying, 'O king Nebuchadnezzar to thee it is spoken, the kingdom is departed from thee, and they shall drive thee from men and thy dwelling shall be with the beast of the field: they shall make thee to eat grass as oxen, and seven times shall pass over thee, until thou know that the Most High ruleth in the kingdom of men and giveth it to whomsoever He will". Daniel 4:29-32

This example in the book of Daniel expresses to us very strongly, that God will not share His glory with any other. In the 1980's at the height of televangelist popularity, and the building of personal empires at the cost of the sanctity of the Gospel truth, morality was sacrificed on the altar of human achievement and fame, and individual ostentation took centre stage. God by His Holy Spirit moved on the stage of human idiosyncrasy and in the arena of human frailty to shake the empires of many of Christendom's famous media heroes, shattering the images of the mini-stars of the Church who at that period reviled the Holly Wood movie stars. Once again God made it clear that He will not share His glory with any other.

In the words of Nebuchadnezzar in Daniel 4:3

"How great are his signs; and how mighty are his wonders His kingdom and His dominion is from generation to generation".

After the humiliating experience of king Nebuchadnezzar of Babylon in

Daniel 4:34

"And at the end of the days I Nebuchadnezzar lifted up nine eyes unto heaven and mine understanding returned unto me and I blessed the Most High, and praised and honored Him that liveth, forever whose dominion is an everlasting dominion and His kingdom is from generation to generation"

Daniel 4:37

"Now I Nebuchadnezzar praise and extol and honor the King of heaven all whose works are truth and His ways judgment. And those that walk in pride He is able to abase"

One of the challenges of successful ministers and ministries is pride. In my Christian experience over the years I have seen many morally right, ethically sound, financial persons who were not moved by the temptation to fall into extra marital relationships; neither did they covet money or fortune. However I have seen those same great men of God fall because of pride. The scriptures remind us that, "Pride goeth before a fall". We are also asked to, "Humble ourselves under the mighty hand of God and he will exalt you in due time". James 4:6, 10

Since the Kingdom rule and authority belongs to God, we need to acknowledge Him every minute of our lives, giving Him glory that is due to His name. Human error which leads to prideful outlook on life has devastated many powerful and purposeful destiny driven people.

Out of the many tragic examples of failure through pride, one stands out in my mind. I once enjoyed the company of a close friend who was extremely talented. He was a guitar player, an influential speaker who was very convincing in the presentation of his conviction and ideas, his devotion to God and the things of God. It was fascinating; this tremendous young man was an encouraging example in the area of praying and fasting. His fervency and articulation in his prayer times were admirable.

His call and gifts were vividly apparent. He was very committed to the development of others and it seemed by all accounts he was destined, to make a sterling contribution to the work of God in his nation. Not forgetting that natural and spiritual favour seemed to follow him, many persons sounded his praise aloud. This young man was privileged to have attended one of Dr. Morris Cerulo's Schools of Ministries in San Diego California U.S.A. for three months after which, he ministered in the USA. Upon his returned home he was sullen with pride, and arrogantly he refused ministry opportunities that were offered to him.

In his quest for the top he made an infamous statement I will never forget, "By the hook or by the crock I will be a leader". This statement of arrogance seems to have propelled him to a slippery slope of self-destruction, rejecting all human efforts of counsel and advice. He lost his wife, became a religious fanatic, opened himself to many erroneous teachings, and lost his sanity—so much so that he was found preaching in a city in the nude at one time. He was eventually placed in a mental institution. Today this man is an aimless wonderer, who seems to have no hope, no goals (pride goes before a fall).

Satan will always try to lead human beings down the same path of his arrogant failure. In the books of Isaiah chapter 14; and Ezekiel chapter 28, the fall of Satan is highlighted. Many of God's people and in particular his anointed ministers, fall to the deception of self glory. We must remind ourselves that the glory belongs to El Elyon the Highest God. There are too many praise stealers in the Church. They are those who refuse to humble themselves and give all the glory to Almighty God, forgetting that every good and perfect gift comes from the Father above. Every gift, talent or ability, is from God who gives to every man severally as He wills, as stated in 1 Corinthians 12:11

> "But all these worketh that one and the selfsame Spirit, dividing to every man severally as He will".

To avoid the destruction of pride and arrogance, there is a need for understanding the functions of the spiritual body (the body of Christ, the called-out ones, the ecclesia, the living spiritual organism), in parallel to the physical body, recognizing that each joint must supply.

The Apostle Paul, writes in the book of Romans, chapter twelve that we should not think higher than we ought to, because god has dealt to every man a measure of faith, emphasizing that whatever gifting that one operates in he or she should minister according to the measure of faith, given to him or her.

The Prophet Isaiah wrote to a rebellious, stiff-necked Israel, who would not turn from their sinful ways by "humbling themselves and walking in obedience to divine will and purpose, saying that God Almighty, the High and Lofty One dwells in a high and lofty place with him that is of a broken and contrite Spirit, to revive the spirit of the humble and revive the spirit of the contrite ones." Isaiah 57:15.

The dismal failure of both man and angels seems to strongly suggest that for us to excel in God and to dwell with Him, we must humble ourselves in reverential fear, recognizing that He God is the only pointate King of the universe, who rules in heaven and in earth, as supreme ruler and the *Master that entire he surveys. The human race with all its ideas and ambitions are reminded in the following scriptures:

Psalms 24: 1-2

"The earth is the Lord's and the fullness thereof; the world, and they that dwell therein; for He founded it upon the seas, and established it upon the floods".

Isaiah 42: 8

"I am the Lord that is my name and my glory will I not give to another, neither my praise to graven images".

In humble adoration we must recognized our position as God's children but also His servants, subjects of the Eternal King and stewards of His manifold grace. Jesus in the model of prayer in Matthew six, which according to Bishop Tudor Bismark of Harare, Zimbabwe, in the southern region of the continent of Africa are six steps to the throne,

1.	Starting with praise:	Our Father which art in heaven hallowed is Thy name;
2.	Priority:	Thy Kingdom come Thy will be done;
3.	Petitions:	Give us this day our daily bread;
4.	Purity:	Forgive us our debts as we forgive our debtor;
5.	Protection:	Lead us not into temptation but deliverer us from evil;
6.	Power:	For Thine is the Kingdom, power and glory forever and ever, everything belongs to God Almighty.

Chapter 7

A Divided Kingdom
From Patriarchal to Kingdom

So Israel rebelled against the house of David unto this day (1 Kings 12:31, 1 Kings 12:19).

Patriarchal to Kingdom:

In this Chapter we will see movement that re-establishes God's original authority structure of Kingdom rule in the earth, through a patriarchal line of Abraham to the kingly line of David.

God has always ordained that man would have dominion or kingship over the earth. The first human beings on earth were made in the likeness of God and given dominion.

Genesis 1:26

"And God said, Let Us make mankind in Our image, after Our likeness, and let them have dominion over [sovereign or supreme authority; the power of governing and controlling]."

Adams federal headship lost through Satanic Schemes:

In Adam's position as a king, he chose to disobey God by listening to the voice of satanic lies, whose intention was to bring a snare to the soul of man. With universal rule as Satan's quest and being its original intent,

Isaiah 14:13

"For thou hast said in thine heart, I will ascend into heaven, I will exalt my throne above the stars of God: I will sit also upon the mount of the congregation, in the sides of the north".

God Almighty banished Lucifer from heaven, and condemned him to eternal judgment by fire. Lucifer became Satan, the ancient dragon, the deceiver, the accuser of the brethren and stole man's kingly position through deception.

Jezebel the epitome of adulterous witchcraft must be examined because the spirit that controlled her sought to destroy God's priestly, prophetic, righteous, kingly rule in the earth, and divided the kingdom of Israel; the people called to be a kingdom of priests. This anti-God spirit launched a diabolic systematic Persecution of Yahweh's Prophets: she brought the worship of the Phoenician Baal and Astarte with her into Hebrew life.

In Revelation 2:20 her lax principles or tendencies made for a connection with foreign and compromising associations which evidently exerted a dangerous influence upon some weaker Christians in the Church. Her followers "prided themselves upon their enlightened liberalism" Revelation 2:24. Today in the Church this spirit is still at work, kill and stifling the priestly and kingly anointing, preventing the Church from arriving and attaining to Kingdom life. The leadership of the Jews in Jesus' day pride themselves of their patriarchal connection to Abraham, but disregards Jesus' kingly anointing. Jesus said that they belong to Satan who was indeed their father, because he sought to kill him. It is also evident in the Church that this spirit is working at dividing the dogmatic philosophical position of the Church, creating a sharp contrast between those who accept son-ship but reject kingship, and those who hang everything on establishing kingship without servant-hood.

In this book we will not be seeking to give a full definition of Jezebel, but just to mention, **Jezebel means: Chaste—virtuous, pure in thought or conduct.**

> **JEZ'EBEL**, n. An impudent, daring, vicious woman. Impudent (marked by audacity, impertinent, disrespectful or insolent-rude insulting) bold; vicious: the ability to impair the use or value of, to render weak or ineffective, to make legally invalid. Daughter of Eth-Baal king of the Zidonians.

This spirit along with the python spirit is rendering the Church weak like it did in the Old Testament. Let us as children of God refuse the reign of that false anti-righteousness demonic spirit in our lives, Church and organizations.

Sins of the fathers:

We are told that the fall of great men, empires or church systems, is through women or opposite sex, pride and money. The kingdom of Israel, was divided by the lust for beautiful women which was a sin that passed down through patriarchal line. The wisest king in Israel's history fell prey to the lustful spirit.

> 1 Kings 11:1
>
> "But King Solomon loved many strange women, together with the daughter of Pharaoh, women of the Moabites, Ammonites, Edomites, Zidonians, *and* Hittites;
>
> 1 Kings 11:5
>
> "For Solomon went after Ashtoreth the goddess of the Zidonians, and after Milcom the abomination of the Ammonites".

The idolatry, into which Solomon fell in his old age, appears so strange in a king so wise and God-fearing as Solomon showed himself to be at the dedication of the temple. It must be noted that great wisdom and a refined knowledge of God are not a defense against the folly of idolatry, since it has its roots in the heart, and springs from sensual desires and the lust of the flesh. One must guard their heart, meditate on the Word of God, and walk circumspectly in holiness, understanding that false compassion mixed with lust, can lead you under the power of the spirit of Jezebel to destroy lives, marriages, churches, ministries and kingdoms.

Sins of Wisdom:

From the earliest years of his reign Solomon was in danger of falling into idolatry. This danger indeed spring in his case from his inclination to foreign customs. We must always understand that leaning on our own understanding, can lead us into destruction and can abort our destiny. Solomon's wives lead him to worship strange gods like Astarte, the chief female deity of all the Canaanitish tribes. Her worship was also transplanted from Tyre to Carthage, where it flourished greatly. She was a moon-goddess, whom the Greeks and Romans called sometimes Aphrodite, sometimes Urania (Σεληναίη).

Idolatrous worship of other gods:

Chemosh: The destroyer, subduwer, or fishgod, the god of the Moabites (Numbers 21:29; Jeremiah 48:7, Jeremiah 48:13, Jeremiah 48:46). The worship of this god, "the abomination of Moab," was introduced at Jerusalem by Solomon (1 Kings 11:7);

Ashtoreth: Is Astarte, the same with the Venus of the Greeks, she was the Ishtar of the Acadians and the Astarte of the Greeks (Jeremiah 44:17; 1 Kings 11:5, 1 Kings 11:33; 2 Kings 23:13)

The Fire Ritual, an Abomination:

Leviticus 18:21

"Thou shalt not let any of thy seed pass through the fire to Molech, etc.

'Molech' or 'Moloch' which signifies "king," was the idol of the Ammonites. Milcom is Molech calf-head god; children were dedicated to this god through a fire ritual.

Federal Headship lost through the worship of Power, Material, Humanism:

Satan envied the Kingdom that God gave to Adam and Eve. Satan's nature involves Liar, Deceiver, Accuser and Thief.

John 10:10

"The thief cometh not, but for to steal, and to kill, and to destroy."

That is his first and principal view; to steal: is to invade, seize, and carry away another's property.

John 8:44

"Ye are of *your* father the devil, and the lusts of your father ye will do. He was a murderer from the beginning, and abode not in the truth, because there is no truth in him. When he speaketh a lie, he speaketh of his own: for he is a liar, and the father of it."

The Federal head pays the Consequence of Rebellion:

Genesis 3:23

"Therefore the LORD God sent him forth from the garden of Eden, to till the ground from whence he was taken."

Genesis 3:24

"So he drove out the man; and he placed at the east of the garden of Eden Cherubims, and a flaming sword which turned every way, to keep the way of the tree of life".

Patriarchal to Kingdom:

Israel, a national movement, started with the principle of faith. God identifies a man on earth to have dominion (through the principle of faith). God gave him a promise.

Genesis 12:1

"Now the LORD had said unto Abram, 'Get thee out of thy country, and from thy kindred, and from thy father's house, unto a land that I will show thee'."

A Kingdom Promise "And I will make thee a great nation":

"and I will bless thee, and make thy name great; and thou shalt be a blessing".

Genesis 12:3

"And I will bless them that bless thee, and curse him that curseth thee: and in thee shall all families of the earth be blessed".

The faith of Abraham elevated him from being ordinary to dominion authority.

God Established Isaac through Obedience:

God used the passion and desire of Jacob. Out of distortion and deception, God builds a wholesome nation through Jacob who became a prince with God. Out of brokenness came a kingdom.

Genesis 32:27

"And he said unto him, 'What *is* thy name? And he said, 'Jacob'."

Genesis 32:28

"And he said, Thy name shall be called no more Jacob, but Israel: for as a prince hast thou power with God and with men, and hast prevailed."

National Kingdom Israel:

Twelve tribes and twelve princes; a kingdom is established. God Who is King, invites princes to reign as king.

Exodus 19:5

"Now therefore, if ye will obey My voice indeed, and keep My covenant, then ye shall be a peculiar treasure unto Me above all people: for all the earth *is* mine:"

Exodus 19:6

"And ye shall be unto me a Kingdom of priests, and a holy nation."

The Name Israel:

The name Israel came out of divine promise and the ardent desire of a man to move from the ordinary to a kingly position.

In the definition, the name Israel gives us this understanding: "He will rule as God".

The name was conferred on Jacob after the great prayer-struggle at Peniel (Genesis 32:28) because "as a prince he had power with God and prevailed. 'Who prevails with God'—Israel is a symbolic name of Jacob. Since Jesus' victorious work on the cross, where He spoilt principalities and powers, destroying Satan-the one who had power over death, He has given the called out ones power through the keys of the Kingdom, to establish the rule of God on earth. Since King Jesus has triumphed, we must not operate as a divided Kingdom but as unified Kingdom under the leadership of the head of the Church, Jesus Christ the conquering Lion of the Tribe of Judah. The Church must not be ignorant concerning the devises of the enemy, in his aim to continue his stealing, killing and destroying of the children of God, holding them back from Kingdom living.

Chapter 8

Kingdom Possessors

"But the saints of the Most High shall take the kingdom, and possess the kingdom forever, even forever and ever". Daniel 7:18

The final battle of the Universe:

There is conspiracy going on in the earth, to over-throw the Kingdom of Light. The Kingdom of Light which is within man lighting the world is under constant attack, since the victorious triumph of Jesus Christ on the cross.

Colossians 2:15

"And having spoiled principalities and powers, he made a show of them openly, triumphing over them in it".

Satan is preparing for the Final Conquest:

The mystery of the age is revealed in Christ which was hidden in God. Jesus Christ on earth reveals the Father, the Spirit of Truth, the unity of God, challenges the spirit of the world, unmasks the antichrist, and exposes the religious spirit. Jesus in Matthew 24 reveals the satanic strategy that is destined to bring chaos through the following:

1. Deception—False prophets and religious compromisers within the visible church;

2. Increase of war, famines and earthquakes;
3. Severe persecution of God's people;
4. Forsaking of loyalty to Christ;
5. In the final quest for global dominance Satan is stir and releasing an avalanche of violence, crime and disregard for God's law rapidly;
6. Decrease in natural love and family affection;
7. Religious deception rampant on earth;
8. Increase of wickedness;
9. An unbelievable increase in immorality;
10. Shamelessness rebellion against God and a throwing off of moral restraint.

Sexual perversion, immorality, adultery, pornography, drugs, ungodly music and lustful entertainment will abound as in the days of Noah.

The Prophet Daniel's Last day's vision:

Daniel 7:2-24
Four great beasts coming on the global scene; the stage is set; the last four kingdoms to rule earth are revealed:

- The Lion king of the jungle: A symbol of royal power, representing the Neo-Babylonian Empire;
- The Eagle the king of birds: King Nebuchadnezzar's power;
- The Bear: Mede-Persia with Persia dominating Media. Ribs in the mouth represent conquest of Babylon, Lydia and Egypt;

- Leopard:　A powerful, swift animal —Alexander's Greek empire,four heads is four kingdoms that came out of his empire. The fourth beast represents Rome, dreadful and terrible reign with iron teeth.

The mystery of iniquity reveals

1 John 2:18

The little horns—the last great Gentile ruler in the world is revealed, the antichrist, that spirit of the age already working in the children of iniquity;

2 Thessalonians 2: 3, 8

The man of lawlessness, Satan's son of perdition is revealed who will wage war against God's saints, speak against God, that spirit of blasphemy will exalt himself as god, seeking to solidify his kingdom over the entire earth realm.

But the saints of the Kingdom will overcome him as they climb and position themselves of the seven building blocks of society, popularly called the seven mountains. Isaiah and the saints will possess the kingdom; in the final analysis the antichrist's kingdom will be destroyed and the kingdom of this world shall be come the kingdom of our Lord and of His Christ.

The Ancient of Days ruling in majestic splendor:

The Eternal:　The judge of all the earth;
His Holiness revealed:　His clothing white as snow;
His Majesty:　The hair white like wool;

His Fiery Justice: His throne was flamed with fire, and its wheels were all ablaze; the consuming fire that makes His angels Spirit and His minister a flame of fire burning with unquenchable zeal, and power.

The saints receive the Kingdom

To rule and reign with God:

*   Promise possession;
*   Keys of authority given;
*   Join heir privileges;
*   Faithfulness rewarded;
*   Because of their relationship with God;
*   Because they have separated themselves from sin and corruption;
*   They consecrated themselves to the service of worship of God.

A Priest amongst kings; a reward of Righteousness

2 Chronicles 24: 16; 25 "Righteousness exalts a nation but sin is a reproach to all people."

1. The Bible tells us that the sins of the fathers pass down to many generations. In fact to the third and fourth generations;
2. But righteousness goes on to a thousand generations. We are told with regards to leadership that everything rises and falls on leadership. In the home, the nation, the church and community everything rises and falls on leadership;
3. Today in our nation the fear, torment and the carnage that is taking place on our streets, the innocent blood and the blood of vengeance, is a direct result of the failure of leadership, particularly in the home;

4. The Church by its constitution is perfectly configured, equipped and positioned to bring the necessary change that our nation needs at this time;

5. The Church is the pillar of truth in the nation, and it is only truth that can set the captivity free. The Church is lead by Jesus Christ who is the truth, the way and the life;

6. The Church is endowed with the source of light, in the universe. Jehovah God who is light;

7. The Church is equipped with the ultimate power of the universe, the power of the Holy Ghost.

8. The Church is the light of the world shining through the darkness of man's hearts;

9. The Church has the keys of the Kingdom, the ultimate source of power and authority to operate on earth which is backed by God's throne;

10. The Church is equipped with the transforming grace of the Holy Spirit changing lives from glory to glory;

11. God's divine order in the universe is unchangeable: God the Father, God the Son Jesus Christ, the man the head of the home, wife, and children in subjection;

12. Anytime society rejects the structure of God there is chaos;

13. Male leadership is critical for the continuation of God's rulership and dominion on earth;

14. Man, is important in the spreading of God's principles on earth through the family (home) which is the first institution, the Church which is the pillar of truth;

15. Society on a whole, men have a responsibility to God, to spread His rule of righteousness, justice, peace, transforming power, in this present life and leave a legacy to the next generation. Are you ready to rise to the challenge?

We are called to be priests but also to reign as kings. The text before us gives a sobering lesson, that the right attitude, mentality, and behaviour in life will result in great rewards, and that it is not how you began but how you finish. A priest, because of how he lived, was buried amongst kings, whilst a king because of his ungodly lifestyle he was not buried in the tombs of the kings.

2 Chronicles 24:16

"And they buried him in the city of David among the kings, because he had done good in Israel, both toward God and toward His house."

2 Chronicles 24:25

"And when they had departed from him (for they left him in great diseases), his own servants conspired against him for the blood of the sons of Jehoiada the priest, and killed him on his bed, and he died. And they buried him in the city of David, but they did not bury him in the tombs of the kings."

2 Chronicles 24:16

"And they buried him in the city of David among the kings, In honour to him, he having been the preserver of the king, and of the kingdom, and being by marriage a relation of the present king, uncle to him:"

"because he had done good in Israel; in that part of it which belonged to the kingdom of the house of David:"

"both towards God, and towards his house; both for the restoring the pure worship of God, and the repairs of the temple. He also participated in the:"

1. The grooming of a son;
2. The developing a king;
3. Through the power of a priestly anointing:

   - He had done good toward God;
   - And toward God's house;

4. Lead a life of righteousness before God, by the training of the priest. Every father should fulfill his priestly role as a father to his wife and children. In his priestly and kingly role he must:

   - Protect his family, provide for his family, provide guidance, and spiritual leadership;
   - Be a lover—Christ model—Philippians 2:6-10;
   - Love as Christ loves the Church;
   - Love wife and not be harsh with wife—Colossians 3:19;
   - Love and live in an understanding way—1 Peter 7:33;
   - Must be a proper role model to wife and children;
   - Proper social, moral, spiritual development of children;
   - Develop proper sexual identity in children;
   - Development of proper self esteem in children;

God is truly looking for men who will take their priestly positions in the home, Church and society and who will rise as kings with a divine anointing to influence nations to Kingdom living.

Chapter 9

Divine Preservation
Preserved unto destiny in His majestic presence

The book of Jude urges believers to "earnestly contend for the faith which was once delivered unto the saints." (Verse 3 King James Version)

In this lawless and liberal religious age there is a need to stand up for what we believe. The believer cannot afford to be tossed to and fro by every wind of doctrine, and every concept of man that is thrown in their way. There is a demand for us to contend for the faith. The former presidents of the United States of America, one of the most powerful nations on earth, were not afraid to declare their faith in the True and Living God.

The believer in Jehovah should be bold with the faith in the midst of this anti-Christ age. Wherever they are, they should boldly lift up Jesus Christ as King of kings and Lord of lords.

Against the background of the prevailing antinomian teaching, which taught that salvation by grace allows them to sin without condemnation, the Apostle Jude describes these unprincipled men as ungodly and as those who do not have the Spirit of the King of Glory. The Apostle Jude wrote this letter to urgently warn believers about the serious threat of false teachers and their subversive influence within the churches, and to forcefully challenge all true believers to rise up and contend for the faith that was entrusted once for all, to the saints. The Apostle Jude concludes his letter with a crescendo of inspiration. In his benediction in verse twenty-four he wrote,

"Now unto Him that is able to keep you from falling, and to present you faultless before the presence of his glory with exceeding joy." (King James Version)

Every born-again believer should contend for the faith, with the understanding of divine preservation and with the hope of being presented faultless before the King of Glory. We must contend for the faith, but more so seek to establish the Kingdom of God in every stratum of societal life, moving into every world and bringing influence to many.

Chapter 10

An Eagle Mentality
Isaiah 40:31; Psalm 103:5

The writer of the Psalms notes that the persons who dwell in the House of the Lord shall progress from strength to strength in the presence of Almighty God.

Psalm 84:4-7

"Blessed are they that dwell in thy house: they will be still praising thee. Selah. Blessed is the man whose strength is in thee; in whose heart are the ways of them. Who passing through the valley of Baca make it a well; the rain also filleth the pools. They go from strength to strength; every one of them in Zion appeareth before God".

There are various Types of People in the Kingdom:

1. You have optimist or pessimist;
2. You have murmuring people or 'praise-rs';
3. You have goat Christians always booting or sheep ready to follow;
4. Men pleasers and God pleasers;
5. Religious believers and believing believers;
6. Rebellion/witchcraft spirit or willing and obedient spirit;

The Church is also filled with all Kinds of People:

1. We have chicken Christians who are afraid of their skin, and allow people to disrespect them, the church and its leadership;
2. Then you have turkey Christians; all their can do is chuckle, and look down;
3. However, there are a few Christians I characterize as eagles that are focused, visionaries, and single minded.

Every believer must decide for themselves on what side of the fence they are going to be. They must choose what type of Christian they are going to be; church goers, fearful, intimidated, underachiever, murmuring, religious, unprogressive, or a Kingdom thinker and dweller.

Those Closest to you will Determine the Level of your Success:

If you hang around losers, you will always be a loser even though you may have goals and guts. There is a vision focus for this Church out of Isaiah 54:2

> "Enlarge the place of thy tent, and let them stretch forth the curtains of thine habitations: spare not, lengthen thy cords, and strengthen thy stakes";

Isaiah 54:3

> "For thou shalt break forth on the right hand and on the left";

Eagle Christians will seek to Advance the Kingdom:

*   They are not so concerned about position but rather the will of God;

- They are committed and faithful;
- Turkeys always show up, but you have to look for eagles, they are busy soaring to higher heights;
- An eagle never has to look for a job; you see an eagle and you see people around him. He or she is a leader.

Dr. John Maxwell said the reasons why some people do not achieve are:

1. It is easier to settle for average than it is to strive for achievement;
2. It is easier to be saturated with complacency than to stir with compassion;
3. It is easier to be skeptical than to be successful;
4. It is easier to question than to conquer;
5. It is easier to rationalize your disappointment than to realize your dreams.

Marks of an Eagle:

- Eagles make things happen; if you put an eagle anywhere, any place, anytime and something positive begins to happen;
- They change the situation for the better;
- Eagles only hang around eagles;
- An eagle does not make a small job a big job, that is the work of turkeys;
- Eagles see opportunities and seize them;
- Eagles influence the opinions and the actions of others for good;
- An eagle adds value to you and the Church.

We are told that there are Four Kinds of People in our Lives:

1. Those who add to your life and ministry;

2. Those who subtract from your life and ministry;
3. Those who divide your life and ministry;
4. Those who multiply your life and ministry;

Anyone who walks with you does one of these four things in your presence. Those who do not increase you will no doubt decrease you.

How do Eagles add Value to your Life?

1. They love their leader unconditionally, they are ready to die for that leader; are with him intentionally, in heart and soul, not based on a position;
2. They make the leader's vision become their vision;
3. The eagle will be faithful in his leader's ministry not his own.

An Eagle Transfers the Loyalty of others to the set man:

- Eagles draw eagles to them; turkeys draw turkeys;
- They give glory to God;
- Portray an image for the glory of His Name;
- Provide quality leadership;
- Provide you with purpose;
- Eagles equip eagles to lead.

Eagles Provide Ideas that help your Ministry or Organization:

1. Eagles possess an uncommonly great attitude;
2. Eagles live up to their commitments;
3. Eagles show fierce loyalty;
4. Eagles re-motivate themselves, "They shall put forth fresh feathers as eagles" are said to renovate themselves.

The Eagle Operates from a High Position:

The Jews have a notion, that for ten years the eagle ascends very high in the firmament of heaven, and approaching near to the heat of the sun. After, it falls into the sea through the vehemence of the heat and then it casts its feathers. Hiding in a cleft of a rock, it waits for new feathers to grow. During this time, it is strengthened, renewed, its feathers grow, and it returns to the days of its youth. So every ten years to a hundred; and in the hundredth year it ascends according to its custom, and falls into the sea, and dies.

Christians with Kingdom mentality are like the eagle.

God satisfies the Longing Soul:

1. Psalm 103:5;
2. By God's provision, the saint retains a youthful vigor like the eagles, looks as vigorous as an eagle, whose eye can gaze upon the sun, and whose wing can mount above the storm;
3. 'Who satisfieth thy mouth with good things," or rather "*filling* with good thy soul?"

No man is ever filled to satisfaction but a believer, and only God Himself can satisfy even him. People with a kingly mentality are like eagles they soar above life's situations and refuse to be entangled by it affairs, but seek to please Him Who has called him, which the Lord Jesus. Like the early disciples, people with an eagle/kingly mentality drop their former vocation, preoccupations, and choose to take up their cross and follow Jesus Christ, seeking first the Kingdom of God, and His righteousness. Seek for the prosperity of your soul, through intellectual understanding and revelatory knowledge, of the Kingdom of God, being transformed by the renewing of your mind, through the Word of God. The Word of God is able to make one wise; submit your will to the high will, submerge into the universal rule of God, beyond time—into eternity.

Chapter 11

Reaping the Kingdom Harvest

"And Jesus went about all the cities and villages, teaching in their synagogues, and preaching the Gospel of the Kingdom, and healing every sickness and every disease among the people. But seeing the crowds, He was moved with compassion on them, because they were tired and scattered like sheep having no shepherd. Then He said to His disciples, 'The harvest truly *is* plenteous, but the labourers are few; therefore pray to the Lord of the harvest that He will send out labourers into His harvest.'" Matthew 9:35-38

The Scriptures tell us that from the days of John the Baptist until now the Kingdom of Heaven has been forcefully advancing and forceful men lay hold on it (Matthew 11:12 NIV). The Amplified Version of this text reads:

> "And from the days of John the Baptist until the present time, the Kingdom of Heaven has endured violent assault, and violent men seize it by force [as a precious prize—a 'share in the heavenly kingdom is sought with most ardent zeal and intense exertion].

We are told by the Apostle Paul that the Kingdom of God is not meat and drink but righteousness, peace and joy in the Holy Ghost (Romans 14:17).

The Kingdom message is geared to bring hope, peace and joy into every dark-confusion, despair, depression, suppression and oppressed situation. The Kingdom of God is light to everyone who finds it.

Reaping the harvest of the Kingdom is every believer's business. Every believer can be a reaper in the Kingdom harvest, as they take heed to the words of the Lord in Matthew 9:35-39.

Jesus' Finished Work:

The finished work of Jesus Christ on the cross is efficacious and truly sets the platform for reaping the harvest of God. The Prophet Isaiah's prediction of the Messiah in Isaiah 60:1a says, "Arise, shine, for the light has come, for the glory of the Lord is risen upon you". This Scripture reveals the power of the Messiah's anointing to break yokes, open blind eyes, set the captives free and introduce us to the transforming power that is available to reap the harvest.

The proclamation of Jesus' ministry in Matthew 1:21, and the definition of His Name, again highlight God's focus on the harvest, "His name shall be called Jesus, because He will save His people from their sins".

Matthew 2:6 foretold that a ruler—a shepherd shall come in the person of Jesus.

> "But you Bethlehem in the land of Judah are by no means least among the rulers of Judah, for out of you will come a ruler who will be the Shepherd of My people Israel".

Jesus spoke of His life as being a provision from God to bring in the harvest in the Kingdom of God,

> "I assure you, most solemnly I tell you, Unless a grain of wheat falls into the earth and dies, it remains [just one grain, it never becomes more but lives] by itself alone. But if it dies, it produces many others and yields a rich harvest." (John 12:24 Amplified Version)

Verse thirty-two of the same chapter says,

"And I, if and when I am lifted up from the earth [on the cross], I will draw and attract all men [Gentiles as well as Jews] to Myself ".

Jesus' announcement of His finished work on the cross in the book of John 19:30, is another indicator of the provision that He made through His sacrificial offering of His life,

"When He had received the drink, Jesus said, 'It is finished.' With that, He bowed His head and gave up His Spirit".

The statement, "it is finished", is inclusive of the fact that Jesus' sufferings in providing redemption for fallen humanity was over and His work of redemption complete. He had borne the punishment for our sins and opened the way of salvation for all. His resurrection pronouncement in Mathew 28:18, Jesus approached the disciples and breaking the silence He said,

"All power is given (all authority, all power and rule) in heaven and on earth has been given unto Me."

Paul's statement of fact, in Colossians 2:15,

"God disarmed principalities and powers that were ranged against us and made a bold display and public example of them, in triumphing over them in Him and in it [the cross]. Amplified Version

The Apostle Paul makes a statement which denotes victory in Romans 8:37. He declares,

"Nay in all these things we are more than conqueror through him that loves us".

To the Hebrews He declares that through the death Jesus, He brought to nought and made of no effect him who had the power over death—that is the devil—that He might deliver completely, all those who, through the haunting fear of death were held in bondage throughout the whole course of their lives. Jesus did a finished and complete work of deliverance as it is written in John 8:36, "Who the Son sets free is free in deed".

The Kingdom of God is defined, from the Greek word "basilica" (denotes sovereignty, royal power, dominion; denoting territory or people over whom a king rules), then the Kingdom of God is:

1. The sphere of God's rule (this earth is largely a scene of universal rebellion against God);
2. The sphere in which, at any given time His (God's) rule is acknowledged.

Throughout the Holy scripture God (Jehovah) calls upon men everywhere without distinction of race or nationality, to submit voluntarily to His rule. The fundamental principles of the Kingdom is declared in the words of the Lord Jesus Christ, spoken in the midst of a company of Pharisees; "The kingdom of God is in the midst of you" (Luke 17:21)

Where the King is, there is the Kingdom. Where the King is and His rule is acknowledged. The Kingdom of God is present, but the Kingdom of God on earth is first within the hearts of individuals.

Acts 4:19

"But Peter and John answered and said to them, Whether it is right before God to listen to you more than to God, you judge, for we cannot but speak the things which we have seen and heard".

The Nature of the Kingdom:

In this discussion, the nature of the Kingdom must be established and put into context in our consideration of reaping the Kingdom harvest. The Kingdom of God or Heaven carries the idea of God coming into the world to assert His power, glory, and dethrone Satan's dominion. The Kingdom of God is primarily an assertion of divine power on earth. Spiritually this rule began on earth in the hearts of men based on the concepts of love, fellowship and divine relationship. John 14:23; 20:22

This breaking into the world and the hearts of men with divine power involves,

1. Spiritual power over Satan's rule and dominion;
2. Power to work miracles and to heal the sick, Mathew 4:23, 9:35;
3. The preaching of the Gospel, accompanied by conversion with regards to sin, righteousness and judgement;
4. The salvation and sanctification of those who repent and believe the Gospel (John 3:3 the new birth)

The Role of the Believers in the Kingdom:

Reaping the harvest of souls is a central role of the believers in the Kingdom. Jesus released the believers to preach the Kingdom, in what He perceived to be an act of reaping the harvest. In Mathew 10:5, the twelve disciples were commissioned, under stark instructions:

> "Jesus sent out these twelve, commanding them saying, 'Do not go into the way of the nations, and do not enter into *any* city of *the* Samaritans. But rather go to the lost sheep of *the* house of Israel'. And as you go, proclaim, saying, 'The Kingdom of Heaven is at hand.' Heal the sick, cleanse the lepers, raise the dead, cast out demons. You have received freely, freely give".

The Harvest is plentiful:

The world is full of people that are out of God's Kingdom, but under the rule of the kingdom of darkness; under Satan's rule. So the harvest is plentiful, as Jesus said, but the labourers are few. Jesus admonishes all believers to remember that the lost have an invaluable everlasting soul, and must spend eternity in heaven or in hell. Jesus did not only send His disciples, but He went through all the towns and villages teaching in their synagogues, preaching the good news of the Kingdom and healing every disease and sickness. Jesus moved with compassion. Compassion is a major factor in reaping the harvest:

Mark 6:34

"And Jesus, when He came out, saw much people, and was moved with *compassion* toward them, because they were as sheep not having a shepherd: and He began to teach them many things." KJV

Matthew 20:34

"So Jesus had *compassion* on them, and *touched* their eyes: and immediately their eyes received sight, and they followed Him." KJV

Mark 1:41

"And Jesus, *moved with compassion*, put forth His hand, and *touched* Him, and saith unto him, 'I will; be thou clean.'" KJV

Mark 5:19

"Howbeit Jesus suffered him not, but saith unto him, 'Go home to thy friends, and tell them how great things the Lord hath done for thee, and hath had *compassion* on thee." KJV

Luke 15:20

"And he arose, and came to his father. But when he was yet a great way off, his father saw him, and had *compassion*, and ran, and *fell on his neck, and kissed him*." KJV

The reaper of the harvest needs compassion for connection. Here are some key facts about compassion. Dr. Pat Glasgow listed these key points:

- Compassion literally is a feeling with and for others;
- It is a fundamental and distinctive quality of the Biblical concept of God;
- It lays at the foundation of Israel's faith in Yahweh;
- It was out of His compassion that He delivered them from Egyptian bondage and called them to be His own people;
- Exodus 34:6 "Yahweh—a God full of compassion and gracious";
- Psalm 86:15 NIV, "But You O Lord, are a compassionate and gracious God, slow to anger, abounding in love and faithfulness."
- Psalm 111:4 NIV, "He has caused His wonders to be remembered; the LORD is gracious and compassionate";
- Psalm 145:8-9 NIV, "The LORD is gracious and compassionate; slow to anger and rich in love. The LORD is good to all; He has compassion on all he has made";
- Lamentations 3:22 NIV, "Because of the LORD's great love we are not consumed, for his compassions never fail";
- The prophets declared that compassion was an essential requirement on the part of members of the community;
- Micah 6:8 NIV, "He has showed you, O man, what is good. And what does the LORD require of you? To act justly, and to love mercy, and to walk humbly with your God";

- Proverbs 19:17 NIV, "He who is kind to the poor lends to the LORD, and he will reward him for what he has done";
- Compassion was an outstanding feature in Jesus Christ (Matt 9:36; 14:14, etc.);
- He taught that it ought to be extended, not to friends and neighbors only, but to all without exception, even to enemies (Matt 5:43-48; Luke 10:30-37);

Luke 10:30-37 Implications are:

1. Compassion is <u>blurred</u> by duties;
2. Compassion is <u>blinded</u> by religious traditions;
3. Compassion can be <u>destroyed</u> by professionalism;
4. Compassion is <u>distorted</u> by ethnic issues (e.g. Peter);
5. Compassion is <u>damaged</u> by selfish interest;
6. Compassion sees men as men—it does not discriminate;
7. Compassion responds to needs;
8. Compassion engages our entire being to act—it sees, hears, acts;
9. Compassion invests time;
10. Compassion invests resources.

We can develop compassion because, it is a human attribute. It is grows with relationship with God. It sharpens when we are in touch with reality. Prayer changes hearts. The harvest belongs to the Lord of the harvest. There are many harvest fields that need someone to reap the Kingdom's harvest and establish the rule of God in the hearts of people. Will you respond to the call to be a reaper of the harvest in expanding the Kingdom of our Kingly Creator?

Chapter 12

The Kingly Creator

The God of all flesh the architect of the age, Creator of heaven and earth is the God who plans, designs and works according to purpose. A group of the intelligentsia within our school of high learning, in their quest to prove that God does not exist in the minds of their followers, have written volumes on evolution, to validate the "Big Bang" theory.

These humanists, evolutionists and so-called educators, have ignored—to their detriment, the Scriptural evidence, alongside the overwhelming facts of nature, and archeological findings, to eloquently articulate that everything around us came into being by accident—what they call the "Big Bang". In their understanding, the "Big Bang" set the course of evolution and this theory tells us that human, plant, marine and animal life are now going through an evolutionary process from one state to another. There is no scientific evidence to prove that through the last six thousand years any evolutionary process has occurred.

The Scriptural declaration of the act of creation is irrefutable through the Scriptural positions of creation which have been put to many historical and scientific tests. The creation position stands true to every examination of Scripture, against historical, archeological, anthropological and scientific scrutiny.

In the beginning of the Bible, it is written in the book of Genesis Chapter One and verse one, that God made the heaven and the earth. The book of Hebrews 11:3 states that the things that are seen were not made by any pre-existing material, but God in Whom all things consist, spoke everything into existence, by the words of His mouth. Just as He thought, He spoke, and what He spoke came into existence as He desired. The account of Genesis along with the Psalms and the articulated, revelatory, position of the Apostle Paul in Romans chapters one and two, indicates that man is without excuse. This is because apart from nature revealing God as Supreme Creator, God Himself has endowed every human-being with intuitive knowledge of the existence of God.

The reality of the situation is that, it does not matter how strong the argument is—the truth remains, God Almighty is unchangeable and He exists. If you are an atheist or a believer in other forms of deity, one day every eye shall see Him and every tongue will confess that Jesus Christ is Lord to the glory of God. The King is coming!

The Presence of a King

In eastern cultures, the king was highly honored and respected. You dared not come into any king's presence unprepared. It was necessary that formal preparation be made because understanding of royal protocol could determine if you live or die. As one approached the king's presence, he or she must bow in adoration and royal salutation. Proper attire and a formal invitation were necessary to get the king's favour. The king's wishes and desires must be paramount in one's mind as he approaches the king.

In modern African countries today, a lot of respect is demanded of tribal chiefs, ministers of government, elders and church leaders. This involves bowing down and prostration, in the presence of human dignitaries. I have said all this to bring to your attention that if earthly kings—mere mortals, who without the shadow of a doubt will die (because their life on earth is short; the Scripture aptly describes it as a vapor that vanishes away; like the grass of the fields, today it is and tomorrow it is not), receives such worship, honour and adoration from their subjects, how much more we should worship, honour and adore God Almighty! In most cases these human dignitaries do not even deserve it because of their wickedness.

Esteemed brother and sister called to be saints, made joint heirs with Jesus Christ, royally chosen and priestly adorned, do you not think the Maker of heaven and earth, the Almighty El Elyon, the Most High God, the I Am that I Am, and the Pontate King of the universe, deserves the best? He deserves our best in worship adoration, protocol, honour and respect.

It is sad to say that the children of God seem to show the greater sense of disrespect and irreverence in their approach and devotion to the Almighty God. In the Body of Christ, many believers approach the Eternal God as if He is a bell hop, a messenger boy, or He is a fast food outlet. We run into His presence to bring our shopping list, and then run back out when things do not go our way. We quickly ask why and even blame God, in utter disrespect, when we fail to receive from God what has nothing to do with Him but our attitude, motives and violation of God's ordained and established principles.

Dear reader, I submit to you that the Almighty God, Ruler of heaven and earth, is worthy of worship. May I remind you that everything we have, gifts, talents, material gain, houses, family, wealth and health are because of Him. We cannot take our next breath without Him. The Apostle Paul in his eloquent and intellectual rebuke to the philosopher of Mars Hills, quotes one of the famous poets saying, "In him we move and our being" (Acts 17:28 paraphrased).

Jesus, in His discourse with the woman at the well in the book of John 4:23 told us that Almighty God—the Father, seeks for worship from true worshippers who will worship the Father in spirit and in truth. Half-hearted devotion, profane worship, worship that is not according to revolutionary truth of Who God is, and worship that does not come out of a pure and true heart shall not be accepted. The Scriptures admonishes us to lift up holy hands without wrath and doubting, in worship to God. Psalm Twenty-Four tells us, the person who shall dwell with God in His tabernacle and courts must have pure hearts and clean hands. Let us approach our King with reverence and adoration, in honour of His name, bowed down, with our hearts in humility and in awe of His majestic splendor, beauty and moral perfection, worshiping Him as the only true and Living God.

Chapter 13

The Elias Company

To the ultimate goal of kingly worship, God is raising what I call an Elias Company. The Elias Company is first of all, believers who have totally committed themselves to the cause of God Almighty. They do not have time with religiosity, hypocrisy, playing church, and church hopping. They are not running after every prophet who comes into town, or have to be in every conference. They are persons with an end-time purpose.

These persons understand that their calling demands consecration and separation. They have no time to play with sin, and they wash their robes white in the Blood of the Lamb. Their conscience is daily sprinkled with clean water as in the book of Ezekiel 36:20-28. Jehovah who is a God of restoration, said through the mouth of the Prophet Ezekiel, that in His ultimate restoration plan for Israel, "He will gather them from the north, and all the countries that they have been driven and He will sprinkle them with clean water; He will take away their stony heart and put a heart of flesh and He will pour His Spirit upon them." Like the children of Israel, the last days' Elias Company shall be set aside for kingly use.

In Israel's history we see Elijah, one of the most prolific prophets of the Old Testament, who is also called Elias in the New Testament. He was totally committed and separated to the cause of God, in a time when Israel was under the leadership of King Ahab, one of the most wicked and godless kings of Israel. He was coupled with his idolatrous wife Jezebel, who led the children of Israel away from God, to worship of Baal. This man of God stood up in Israel by the direction of the Holy Spirit, to declare judgment in the form of a drought for three and a half years. This created such a chaotic situation in Israel causing cannibalism to be practiced so severely, that King Ahab blamed the prophet for the demise of his country, calling Elijah 'the one that troubles Israel'. The prophet remained consecrated and pure, and led a show down between the power of Baal and God Almighty, with the focus of bringing the people back to God.

The prophet had to prepare the hearts of the people to receive their God and King; he was the one who prepared the way of the Lord. To the children of Israel this showdown on Mount Carmel saw the inability of Baal to answer by fire, even though four hundred prophets of Baal cried from morning until evening, cutting themselves relentlessly, and still receiving no answer. Elijah challenged the nation asking them to choose, "Why halt ye between two opinions? If Baal be God then serve him, but if Jehovah be God then serve Him" (1 Kings 18:21), establishing that the god that answers by fire he is God. In the final analysis, after the miserable failure of the prophets of Baal, Elijah builds an altar of stone and drenched the sacrifice and the altar with water. He then called on the God of Heaven, Who answered in a dramatic display of His fire which dried up the water and burned the sacrifice. That day the people of Israel turned back to the true and living God.

The Lord God Almighty was recognized as the only True and Living God. Elijah the prophet prepared the heart of the people to receive their King.

The Elias Company are believers in Jesus Christ as Messiah and Lord, who have a mandate to first of all prepare their own hearts to receive the Lord, and secondly to prepare the hearts of others for the coming of the King (1 Kings 17 and 18).

We are told by the Prophet Malachi, that one of the last days Old Testament prophets will be Elijah.

Malachi 3:1, 2 KJV

"Behold, I will send My messenger, and he shall prepare the way before me: and the Lord, whom ye seek, shall suddenly come to his temple, even the messenger of the covenant, whom ye delight in: behold, he shall come, saith the Lord of Hosts. But who may abide the day of his coming? and who shall stand when he appeareth? For he is like a refiner's fire, and like a fullers' soap;"

Malachi 4:5 KJV

"Behold, I will send you Elijah the prophet before the coming of the great and dreadful day of the Lord:"

Isaiah 40:3-5 KJV

"The voice of him that crieth in the wilderness, 'Prepare ye the way of the Lord, make straight, in the desert a highway for our God. Every valley shall be exalted, and every mountain and hill shall be made low: and the crooked shall be made straight, and the rough places plain: And the glory of the Lord shall be revealed, and all flesh shall see it together: for the mouth of the Lord hath spoken it".

There is a clarion call in Psalm 24:7-10 KJV

"Lift up your heads, O ye gates; and be ye lift up, ye everlasting doors; and the King of glory shall come in. Who is this King of glory? The Lord strong and mighty, the Lord mighty in battle. Lift up your heads, O ye gates; even lift them up, ye everlasting doors; and the King of glory shall come in. Who is this King of glory? The LORD strong and mighty, the LORD mighty in battle. Lift up your heads, O ye gates; even lift them up, ye

everlasting doors; and the King of glory shall come in.
Who is this King of glory? The LORD of Hosts, he is
the King of glory. Selah"

As we look at the aforementioned scriptures, we can draw by
inference that God Almighty, the King of glory will not come unless
there is adequate preparation for His coming. This draws reference
both to His end time revelation in the rapture in 1 Thessalonians
4:16-18; when He comes in the clouds to meet His Bride and His
second coming, when He bursts the eastern sky with ten thousand
of ten thousands of His saints, to establish righteousness on earth.
Our present experience is like that of the Church of Revelation in
particular the Laodicea church;

Revelation 3:20

"Behold, I stand at the door, and knock: if any man hear
my voice, and open the door, I will come in to him, and
will sup with him, and he with me."

God's desire is to dwell amongst us and tabernacle with us.
Many times in our Christian experience we find ourselves in a place
of dryness. Some believers even backslide in their hearts, moving
away from God's abundant life but today, it is necessary that we
return to Him so that He can draw close unto us, bringing revival
and times of refreshing to give us spiritual breakthrough that leads
to Kingdom living. As Kingdom people, we need to prepare our
hearts for God to come and visit us. Many Christians have missed
their season and time of divine visitation because of a lack of
preparation. They were not in the place for God's blessing to flow.

The Elias Company are those whose hearts are ready to receive
the King. They have heeded the call of the Psalmist to, "Open ye
gates, ye everlastings doors, and the King of glory shall come in"
(Psalm 24:9). They are those who enter into God's divine presence
and are also committed and devoted to make a path straight for
others.

Lastly the Elias Company, as preparers of the path to dwell in, operate in faith.

James 5:17, 18

"Elias was a man subject to like passions as we are, and he prayed earnestly that it might not rain: and it rained not on the earth by the space of three years and six months. And he prayed again, and the heaven gave rain, and the earth brought forth her fruit."

Signs and wonders follow the Elias Company because of their faith in God. They fearlessly challenge unbelief, religiosity, error, wickedness, and seek to pull out of the fires of hell, those who have been spotted. Jesus said in answer to the Jew's question concerning what the Scripture says about Elias coming in the day of the Lord, "John the Baptist came in the spirit of Elias, the last days' Elias Company walks in the spirit of Elias preparing the way of the King." To be a part of the Elias Company one must operate in Kingdom authority.

Chapter 14

Operating in Kingdom Authority

We are told that the greatest tragedy in life is not sickness or death but it is a life without purpose, without plan, and lead by ignorance. We must constantly be reminded that God made everything on earth with a purpose. God's creative genius, immaculate taste, and beauty, are clearly seen in all that He creates, yet at the same time things on earth were not made just for beauty, but with an intended purpose. Man born of a woman is not void of purpose. We were chosen by God to be on planet earth at this particular time and season. The book of Ecclesiastes chapter three, reminds us that to everything under the sun there is a time and season.

As we seek to identify our specific purpose on earth, we must take a journey to the Book of Genesis in the Bible; because it is there we can clearly understand the mind of the Creator.

Genesis 1:26

"And God said, 'Let us make man in our image, after our likeness: and let them have <u>dominion</u>, over the fish in the sea, and over the fowl of the air, and over the cattle, and over all the earth, and over every creeping thing that creepeth upon the earth."

God said, to let them rule having dominion. It is important to understand at this time, the principle of first things. When God establishes a thing for the first time, it remains a rule of law or a Kingdom governing principle which is locked in divine purpose.

God Almighty created man not only to enjoy that which He had created, but also to have dominion, rulership and authority over the earth. It must be noted that in this present age, God did not give to man rulership in the heavens. It is always God's purpose that man would rule on earth. This created purpose must be understood to operate in Kingdom authority. This position of rule and dominion was hijacked by man's rebellion and greed, and was carelessly given to God's enemy—the enemy of our souls, Satan.

By the revelation of Scriptures, it must be understood that the original purpose of God for man was victoriously restored by Jesus' death on the cross at Calvary. Colossians 2: 15-17 tells us that Jesus

> ". . . spoiled principalities and powers, he made a show
> of them openly, triumphing over them in it . . ."

Jesus arose on resurrection morning after three days and three nights in the belly of the earth, with a triumphant proclamation over death and the grave saying, "All power is given unto me in heaven and in earth" (Mathew 28:18)

The result of man's tragic error and consequences that followed is vividly seen as an imprint through the history of man in the Old Testament, starting with the murder of Abel by his brother Cain in a horrified manner. It continues with the despicable, graphic description of a world gone wild without law and order, driven by a snared conscience and total defiance to God's principles. Genesis chapter six shows us a loving God and Father who is grieved by the sinful, immoral acts of a degenerated man.

God's judgment in Noah's days was a severe flood that brought upon mankind a catastrophe, and cataclysmic phenomena, that the world has never seen since. The entire earth was covered by water, drowning everything in its path except Noah's family of eight and the animals that God had directed him to hand-pick for the continuation of their species. God's judgment is sure, sin will be judged.

Evidently through the Old Testament period we see a power shift. There was a kingdom that had taken hostage the human race, destroying generations after generations through their own ignorance, pride, greed and godlessness. If the Church is to operate effectively in Kingdom authority, it must through the pages of Scripture, identify the hostages taken and understand the sphere of their operation in the sea, earth and air. We are told that Satan (Lucifer) the fallen angel is the prince of the power of the air (Isaiah 14, Ezekiel 28) and that Leviathan is the prince over the children of pride.

The Apostle Paul in the New Testament era enlightened the Ephesians Christians regarding the spiritual warfare that is waged daily, noting that, "We wrestle not against flesh and blood, but against principalities, against powers, against the rulers of the darkness of this world, against spiritual wickedness in high places" (Ephesians 6:12).

The Scripture tells us that the hostage takers have a kingdom based on earth, in the sea and in the air throughout the history of man. Mankind has sought for help and power from what the Scripture calls the kingdom of darkness. This kingdom of darkness cannot be ignored if we are going to successfully operate in our Kingdom authority.

God in His master plan to realign man to his original power and authority base had a fail-proof plan before He established the foundation of the earth. The plan was to redeem man from his fallen hijacked position, through means of redemption. The Scripture describes Jesus as a lamb slain from the foundation of the world. God in His justice dealt with man who fell from grace through disobedience, judging every participant in the conspiracy against God's eternal plan for man on earth. In Genesis chapter three we see God's judgment upon Adam, that "by the sweat of thy brow, through thongs and thistles" and to Eve He said her desire shall be to the man. In essence she shall look to him for leadership, and in pain she shall bring forth children. To the serpent, God spoke a prophetic judgment. He said that, "The seed of the woman shall bruise the head of the serpent (his authority based rulership which he had gained deceptively), and you shall bruise his heel", speaking of the death of Christ on the cross.

Jesus successfully defeated Satan on the cross. This is a mystery hidden from the mystic, deceptive kingdom of darkness, even though many attempts were made throughout the life of the children of Jacob to wipe out any potential seed. Even at time of the birth of Jesus, Herod sent his demolition death squad to kill all Jewish male children born at a certain time.

The Apostle Paul wrote to the Corinthian Christians saying, "If the princes of this world knew they would not have crucified the King of glory" because what they did not know, was that His death would destroy Satan's power—the power of death and hell. The Apostle John wrote in 1 John 3:8

> "He that commits sin is of the devil; for the devil sinneth from the beginning. For this purpose the Son of God was manifested, to destroy the works of the devil"

Dear readers, for us to operate in Kingdom authority, we must claim, appropriate and accept that which was accomplished for us through Jesus Christ, the Son of the Living God.

The Church which God calls out of the worldly system, the "ecclesia", is His demolition army. This "ecclesia" has a mandate to take back from Satan and his kingdom what he took deceptively from mankind. Jesus established Himself as a Good Shepherd, who came to give abundant life. In the book of St. John chapter ten, He said, "The thief comes to steal, kill and destroy but I am come that you might have life and have it more abundantly". We must walk into what Jesus has provided and made possible through His priceless sacrifice.

Jesus Christ with the assurance of victory over the kingdom of darkness boldly declared in Matthew 16:17 after the Apostle Peter received a divine revelation of Who He was, "I am building My Church and the gates of hell shall not prevail against it". This power and authority has been restored to the human race and everyone who is born of God through faith, overcomes the dark world system.

We cannot blame politicians, kings and other authority figures of our world for the chaotic situation. The power to stop and change things is imbedded in the believer. The policing and military power is given to the Church. The responsibility to raise the foundation of many generations which Satan and his army have established over thousands of years can be uprooted and destroyed.

Mathew 16:19

"And I will give you the keys of the kingdom of heaven, and whatever you bind on earth will be bound in heaven, and whatever you loose on earth will be loosed in heaven." NKJV

Mathew 18:18, 19

"Assuredly, I say to you, whatever you bind on earth will be bound in heaven, and whatever you loose on earth will be loosed in heaven. Again I say to you that if two of you agree on earth concerning anything that they ask, it will be done for them by My Father in heaven." NKJV

Awesome authority with responsibility has been bestowed upon the believer, but it must be remembered that the power is not of us but of God. There are foundations that must be raised so that new a foundation can be established in the earth. This is only possible as we understand Kingly authority, first of all in our lives—crowning Jesus Christ as Lord and remaining under God's authority and His humanly appointed authority over you. The Roman centurion of Jesus' days taught us something about authority that we must never forget.

The centurion came to Jesus, for healing of one of his soldiers. Jesus heard his request, and offered to accompany him to bring healing to the sick soldier. The centurion said something that startled Jesus in amazement. He said, "You do not have to come to my house, because I am a man of authority. I say to one come and he comes; and to another go and he goes. Speak the word only and he shall be made whole" (Matthew 8: 5-13 paraphrased). Jesus commended the faith of the centurion as great faith that had not been seen since in all Israel.

If we are going to operate with Kingdom authority, we must be under authority. Operating under authority is a serious issue for the Church; its ministers and members must grapple with this. The authority of God's Kingdom flows through consecrated, submissive vessels. If we the Church have to exhibit God's Kingdom power over the kingdom of darkness, the elements and the circumstances of life, we must be clean. Zechariah Chapter Three from verses one to seven illustrates and depicts a sad situation. Here was Joshua the high priest standing before the Angel of the Lord, and Satan standing at his right hand to resist him. What is note-worthy is that he had filthy garments. In the Chapter, the Angel of the Lord rebuked Satan and ordered that clean garments be put on Joshua. The power of the Holy Ghost flows through clean vessels, also the element of faith is of utmost importance in dealing with the kingdom of darkness.

We must believe that God is all-powerful and the power we have is greater than the power of darkness. We must truly believe, 'greater is He that is in us, than he that is in the world' (1 John 4:4). Lastly, there is a fast that God has ordained to break the bands of wickedness, undo every heavy burden, and set the captive free. The greater our consecration through fasting and prayer, the easier it is for God's power to flow. Whilst Jesus was on earth, His disciples faced the challenge of their life! A father brought his son who was deaf and dumb to be healed but the disciples were not successful. When Jesus arrived on the scene He rebuked their unbelief and said, "These go out not, but by prayer and fasting". Stirrup and exercise the authority and power of God's Kingdom right here on earth by dwelling in the transforming presence of the King!

Chapter 15

In the Presence of the King
The transforming presence of the King.

"Thou wilt show me the path of life: in thy presence *is* fullness of joy; at thy right hand *there are* pleasures forevermore." Psalm 16:11

I remember as a boy of seven years old, the queen of England, Queen Elizabeth II, made a visit to my country. I was an infant, a student at the Roman Catholic Boys' School and I remember the excitement and meticulous preparation we went through. Students from all schools were gathered in an orderly manner on a particular route, waiting for hours with St. Lucian Flags in hand, scourged by the sun (which was extremely hot!). Some students were unable to stand the heat and began to faint; there was a sense of anxiety and restlessness, but yet order was maintained. Suddenly, we could see the motorcade in a distance and as Her Highness' vehicle approached, spontaneously, smiles sighing relief as if to say, 'at last' appeared on our faces! Instantly flags began waving creating a kaleidoscope of colours. The effects of gold, blue, white and black, which was meticulously planned with much anxiety, was gone in a fleeting moment the Queen was here.

History was written, Her Majesty the Queen of England, visited St. Lucia, and I saw her face to face. As I reflect in my adult years, I ask myself the question, "What impact did her visit have on Saint Lucia? After her visit, what changed in Saint Lucia?" As I recall, life continued as usual. In my own personal life, I ask the question, "What impact did the Queen's visit have?" Was my life enriched in any way? As I assess, I must conclude that she had no life changing effect on me.

You cannot be in the presence of the King of kings, and Lord of lords and not be changed for the better!

Psalm 91:1-3

"He that dwelleth in the secret place of the most High shall abide under the shadow of the Almighty. I will say of the LORD, *He is* my refuge and my fortress: my God; in him will I trust. Surely he shall deliver thee from the snare of the fowler, *and* from the noisome pestilence. He shall cover thee with his feathers, and under his wings shalt thou trust: his truth *shall be thy* shield and buckler".

The life-changing effect of being in the presence of God is phenomenal, elated and awesome. The Prophet Isaiah, one of the major prophets of the Old Testament, who covered in his prophetic declaration, Israel's conditions, cause and result of their continuous sinning, predicted an apocalyptic, climatic end of earth's rebellion and God's reign on earth. He had a fascinating experience in the presence of God that was life-changing, God-sensitive, vision-focused, and purpose-directed. In verse one of chapter six of the book of Isaiah; the prophet had a life-changing vision that ushered a celestial plain, that literally transformed him inside out (see Isaiah 6:1-8).

Isaiah 6:1

"In the year that King Uzzaih died I saw also the Lord sitting upon a throne, high and lifted up, and his train filled the temple".

This was a rare human experience to be ushered into God's divine presence. The description of what he saw is still unexplainable by human understanding,

Isaiah 6:2

"Above it stood the seraphims: each one had six wings;
with twain he covered his face and with twain he covered
his feet and with twain he did fly".

The covering of the seraphim indicates that they could not look
at the enthroned presence of God and could not stand naked in His
presence, so they covered their feet.

Isaiah 6:3, 4

"And one cried unto another, and said Holy, holy, holy,
is the Lord of Hosts; the whole earth is full of his glory.
And the posts of the door moved at the voice of him
that cried, and the house was filled with smoke."

Isaiah the Prophet was privileged to see the throne-room of the
King of the universe. No doubt, it was an unexplainable experience
and indescribable sight to him. The effect of God's divine presence
on Isaiah was definitely life-changing and soul reverting. This
propelled him to a place of nothingness; he cried in anguish, of
what he saw—the ventilating but yet light-piercing, love-filled moral
beauty and perfection, in the splendour of His holiness, drawing
him to this conclusion;

"Then said I, Woe is me for I am undone; because I am
a man of unclean lips and dwell in the midst of a people
of unclean lips; for mine eyes have seen the King, the
Lord of Hosts." Isaiah 6:5

In the presence of the King, Isaiah's human fragility and
imperfection was exposed and he saw himself as nothing, and
undone because of God's holiness.

Dear reader, there is a place in God's presence where humanity
dissipates into nothingness and divinity fills all in all. It is there that

the condition of our hearts is revealed: arrogance, malice, jealousy, strife, debates and human pride are exposed in the presence of the Holy One of Israel, which ignites an inner trembling, fear, mixed with despair which drives conviction, that moves us into confession of our sinfulness, demanding repentance—a total turn around into a divinely ordained path. The scripture tells us that where the two's and the three's are gathered in His name there He is to be blessed. This thought is comforting to know, because God is omnipresent, that is, He is everywhere at the same time, that is why we cannot hide from Him.

If we make our bed in hell He is there. He knows and sees all things, which is why He knows the hearts of persons who are genuinely seeking for Him, have love for Him and are committed and consecrated to Him. A prophet of Israel named Samuel, had a rude awakening in Jesse's house. Samuel was commissioned by God to anoint a king from the sons of Jesse to succeed the rejected King Saul. In his human reasoning, Eliab, tall, with well-built, structure qualified him for the kingly position. God intervened and explained to Samuel that man looks on the outside, but God looks at the inside; He sees the deep thoughts. King David in

Psalm 51:6;

"Behold thou desirest truth in the inward parts and in the hidden part thou shalt make me to know wisdom."

God sees deep within us so we should not try to hide our sinful and un-repentant hearts.

What is in our hearts?

There is a much deeper and different experience, when you are in the manifested presence of God. Your religious world is changed, the motives of your heart are revealed, and we are brought to a place of cleansing. Psalms 24:3-5; asks the question,

"Who shall ascend into the hill of the Lord? or who shall stand in his holy place? He that hath clean hands, and a pure heart; who hath not lifted up his soul unto vanity, nor sworn deceitfully. He shall receive the blessing from the Lord, and righteousness from the God of his salvation".

A person cannot enter and leave the manifested presence of the Almighty God untransformed.

After God cleansed Isaiah with a coal of fire from the altar, his spiritual sensitivity was heightened; his ability to hear the voice of God, to hear God's heart beat and receive the burden of the Lord, was at its zenith.

Isaiah 6:8

"Also I heard the voice of the Lord, saying, 'Whom shall I send, and who will go for us?' Then said I, 'Here am I send me'"

There are many believers in the body of Christ who live an aimless life, void of purpose and are unable to sense and discern the move of the Spirit of God. Others live slack lives in sin and immorality, or exist in disobedience and rebellion, or are held hostage by the enemy Satan and his demons. The Church of God definitely needs a visitation of divine presence where the manifested presence of God consumes all impurity and brings supernatural breakthrough and Kingdom life.

Brethren the man Moses who was a type of Christ, was transformed, not just by the knowledge that he was a child of a Hebrew slave. This knowledge drew him to bitterness, and resentment towards the Egyptians who had his people in slavery. It was after Moses had committed the act of murder and ran for his life that God appeared to him in an experience that changed him forever.

Exodus 3:2

"And the angel of the Lord appeared unto him in a flame of fire out of the midst of a bush: and he looked, and, behold, the bush burned with fire, and the bush was not consumed."

God seeing his interest, called unto him,

Exodus 3:4, 5

"And when the Lord saw that he turned aside to see, God called unto him out of the midst of the bush and said, Moses, Moses. And he said here am I. And He said, 'Draw not nigh hither: put off thy shoes from off thy feet, for the place whereon thou standest is holy ground.'"

God made Himself known to Moses as the I Am, that I Am, the Self-existing One. Moses, after that discourse, was changed forever. He found his purpose, and fearlessly challenged Pharaoh and his magicians, subsequently leading the children of Israel out of slavery. Consistently after that first encounter, Moses frequently went into the presence of God so much so; that his very face shone with a dazzling light which demanded that he veiled his face in the presence of the children of Israel.

There is a revolutionary change that takes place, when we spend time in the awesome manifested presence of the King of glory. It is a feeling and position that once you have entered, you cannot live without! There remains with you an increasing desire and longing for more of God's presence. Moses became a God-chaser! In his quest for more of God he requested to see God as he is, unveiled.

King David of Israel cried to see God as He is in the sanctuary. After David's sin of adultery and murder, confronted by Nathan the prophet of God, he repented. In his repentance plea he cried in Psalms 51:11

"Cast me not from thy presence; and take not thy Holy Spirit away from me".

King David cherished the presence of God more than anything else. For us as God's people to flow in Kingdom life, the presence of God must be inhibited by us. We must constantly dwell in His manifested presence. There are many blessings and benefits for the servants of God in this era of grace. The disciples of old both under law and grace experienced the glory of God so mightily. As they passed by, many were slain in God's presence, demon spirits were made uneasy—screaming out of bodies because of the tangible manifested presence of God Almighty, the King of glory. Ephesians 2:22 tells us that the Church is built to house the presence of God earth.

"In whom ye also are builded together for a habitation of God through the Spirit". KJV

Lovers of Jehovah, let us pursue the presence of the King—not just His acts but His presence comes. It is then we shall experience His power, purity, and purpose! It is then that we will experience His Kingdom!

Bibliography

1. Dr. Myles Monroe, In Pursuit of Purpose
2. John Maxwell, Leadership, Laws and Principle
3. Terry L. Gyger
4. W. Barclay
5. Haddon W. Robinson
6. Mac. Arthur F. John Jr.
7. Dr. Bill Hamon, Spiritual Gifts Training Manual
8. Kervin J. Conner
9. Dr. Pat Glasgow, Workshop Document on Reaping the Harvest 2008, Saint Lucia District Conference
10. Bishop Tudor Bismark; Harare, Zimbawe, Spiritual Warfare

Biblical Source

1. New International Version
2. King James Version
3. Amplified Version
4. Life Application Bible, notes on, "King of God, Kingdom of Heaven".